Football School

Name: ....

Class: ....

Coaches: ....

KICKITO ERGO SUM

To BNZ – A.B.

To ABC – B.L.

For my dad – S.G.

First published 2022 by Walker Books Ltd
87 Vauxhall Walk, London SE11 5HJ

2 4 6 8 10 9 7 5 3 1

Text © 2022 Alex Bellos and Ben Lyttleton
Illustrations © 2022 Spike Gerrell

The right of Alex Bellos and Ben Lyttleton, and Spike Gerrell
to be identified as authors and illustrator respectively of this work has been
asserted in accordance with the Copyright, Designs and Patents Act 1988

This book has been typeset in Palatino

Printed and bound by CPI Group (UK) Ltd, Croydon CR0 4YY

British Library Cataloguing in Publication Data:
a catalogue record for this book is available from the British Library

ISBN 978-1-5295-0684-6

www.walker.co.uk
www.footballschool.co

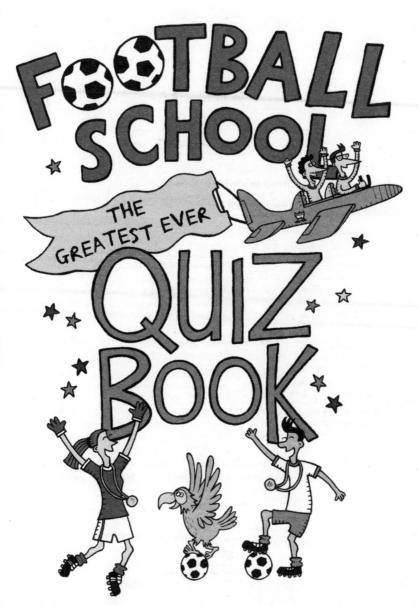

FOOTBALL SCHOOL

THE GREATEST EVER

QUIZ BOOK

Alex Bellos & Ben Lyttleton

Illustrated by Spike Gerrell

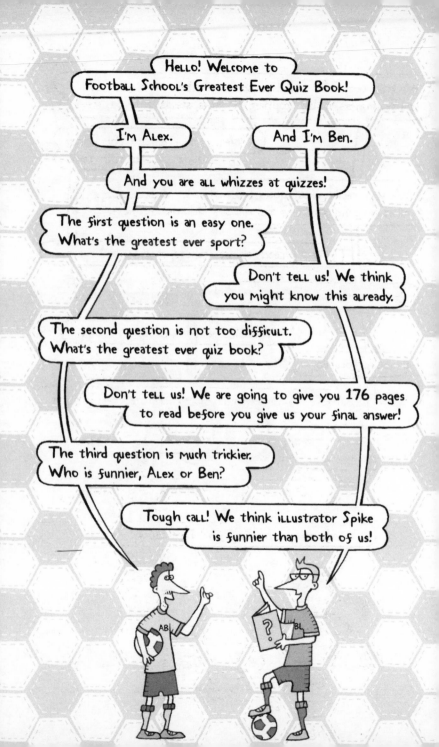

CONTENTS

Look at
our titles!

It's a strong line-up!

GLOBAL GAME

ootball is the game that brings the world together. It's the planet's most popular sport, enjoyed everywhere from Albania to Zimbabwe. Hundreds of millions of people play the game and billions follow it on TV. If you are reading this book, we guess you like to play and watch too!

We're going to begin this book with some history and geography. Humans have been playing ball games for thousands of years, but modern football only emerged in Britain about 150 years ago when rules were agreed on how to distinguish it from rugby and other sports. Not long after, the game spread to Europe and then across the seas to other continents.

In 1904, a group of football lovers in Paris founded the Fédération Internationale de Football Association, or FIFA, in order to organize international matches. The game was now poised to take over the world. And it did! A century later, every country in the world has a football league, and every country has a national team (with the exception of some tiny islands in the Pacific). More than half the world's population aged four and above watched the last World Cup. Unbelievable!

Football has become more than just a sport: it's a language, a culture, a communal experience that is shared and enjoyed across the world. It truly is the global game!

1. **Below we have listed thirteen countries together with football facts about them. They also form an acrostic of THE GLOBAL GAME. Find each country on the map:**

COUNTRIES	FACTS
Trinidad and Tobago	Smallest country to qualify for a World Cup until 2018
Hungary	1954 World Cup runners-up
Egypt	Most victories at Africa Cup of Nations
Germany	Four-time World Cup winners
Liberia	Former Ballon D'Or winner George Weah elected president
Oman	Two-time winners of the Gulf Cup
Bolivia	Highest national stadium in the world
Algeria	Africa Cup of Nations winners in 1990 and 2019
Laos	National team's nickname is Power of the Children of Sticky Rice
Ghana	World Cup quarter-finalists 2010
Argentina	World Cup winners 1978 and 1986
Mexico	World Cup hosts in 1970 and 1986
England	World Cup winners 1966

2. **The ball game *cuju* was played in China and Korea from around 200 BC to AD 1400. In one version of *cuju*, players in long robes aimed to kick a ball through a hole in a sheet attached between two bamboo posts. Winners won silver bowls but what happened to the losing players?**

a) They were beheaded.

b) They had to work as servants for the winning players for a year.

c) They were given wooden bowls.

d) Their faces were smeared with white powder and they were whipped in public.

3. **During medieval times in Britain, "mob football" was a popular pastime. Matches involved two teams – each with an unlimited number of players – and a ball. Each side battled to take the ball to opposing sides of a field or village. In 1477, King Edward IV of England banned mob football because he wanted Englishmen to practise which other sport?**

a) Archery

b) Rugby

c) Jousting

d) Basketball

4. The Football Association was founded in 1863 in order to agree a set of common rules for the sport. Which three of the following six rules were included in the first-ever laws of the game?

a) Players can catch the ball.
b) Players can pick up the ball from the ground.
c) Players can throw the ball.
d) A goal is scored when the ball passes between the posts at whatever height.
e) Teams swap sides after every goal.
f) Players can have studs on their boots.

5. A match between Scotland and England which took place in Glasgow in 1872 is recognized as the first-ever international football match. What was the score?

a) Scotland 6–4 England
b) Scotland 1–7 England
c) Scotland 0–0 England
d) Scotland 10–0 England

6. What was the name of the Frenchman who was FIFA president between 1921 and 1954, and who is known as the father of the World Cup? He had served as a soldier in the First World War and hoped that the competition would promote cooperation and friendliness between nations. The first World Cup trophy was named after him.

a) Just Fontaine
b) Charles de Gaulle
c) Coupe du Monde
d) Jules Rimet

7. In 1930, the inaugural World Cup involved fourteen nations from three continents: Europe, North America and South America. Who were the first countries from Africa, Asia and Oceania to play in a World Cup?

	AFRICA	ASIA	OCEANIA
a)	Egypt	South Korea	Australia
b)	Nigeria	China	Fiji
c)	Cameroon	Japan	New Zealand
d)	Morocco	Saudi Arabia	Tonga

8. The following cities have all hosted games in either the Men's or Women's World Cups. Can you match them to their countries?

CITY		COUNTRY	
a)	Busan	1)	Brazil
b)	Durban	2)	Canada
c)	Kazan	3)	China
d)	Kaiserslautern	4)	France
e)	Manaus	5)	Germany
f)	Orlando	6)	Italy
g)	Palermo	7)	Russia
h)	Toulouse	8)	South Africa
i)	Winnipeg	9)	South Korea
j)	Wuhan	10)	USA

9. **Players from 113 different countries have played in the Premier League since it began in 1992. In 2020, Aston Villa striker Mbwana Samatta became the player from the 100th different country to score in the Premier League. What country is he from?**

   a) Cuba
   b) Mauritania
   c) Tanzania
   d) Barbados

10. **Football is played all across the world! Name the football club whose home town (in brackets) is nearest to each of the following geographical features.**

    North Pole:
    a) Alaska Timbers (Anchorage, USA)
    b) KR (Reykjavík, Iceland)
    c) FC Santa Claus (Rovaniemi, Finland)
    d) Tromsø IL (Tromsø, Norway)

    Equator:
    a) Barcelona SC (Guayaquil, Ecuador)
    b) Coton Sport FC (Garoua, Cameroon)
    c) Enyimba (Aba, Nigeria)
    d) Millonarios (Bogotá, Colombia)

    South Pole:
    a) Deportes Puerto Montt (Puerto Montt, Chile)
    b) Guillermo Brown (Puerto Madryn, Argentina)
    c) Orlando Pirates (Johannesburg, South Africa)
    d) Southern United (Otago, New Zealand)

11. **FIFA recognizes 211 member countries, meaning that these 211 are all able to enter the qualification rounds of the World Cup. Which five of the men's teams below are recognized by FIFA and therefore play in World Cup qualifiers? (Not all of the names below are countries!)**

a) Andorra

b) Bahamas

c) Cornwall

d) Gibraltar

e) Greenland

f) Kosovo

g) South Sudan

h) Tibet

i) Vatican City

j) Zanzibar

12. **What is the only country to have won both the men's and the Women's World Cup?**

a) Argentina

b) Brazil

c) France

d) Germany

13. **Can you match the international players below to the country in which they were born? In each case, they play for a different national team (in brackets) than their birth country, either because they lived in the new country for a long time, or because their parents or grandparents are from the new country.**

PLAYER	COUNTRY
a) Raheem Sterling (England)	1) USA
b) Ché Adams (Scotland)	2) Democratic Republic of Congo
c) Jorginho (Italy)	3) Ghana
d) Alphonso Davies (Canada)	4) Brazil
e) Christian Benteke (Belgium)	5) England
f) María Sánchez (Mexico)	6) Jamaica

14. **Each continent has its own international tournament. Which teams have won their continental competitions the most times?**

Europe – Euros
a) Spain
b) Italy
c) West Germany
d) Germany

Africa – Africa Cup of Nations
a) Algeria
b) Cameroon
c) Egypt
d) Ghana

South America – Copa América
Two of these countries are tied for most wins
a) Chile
b) Argentina
c) Brazil
d) Uruguay

North America – Gold Cup
a) Canada
b) USA
c) Mexico
d) Costa Rica

Asia – Asian Cup
a) South Korea
b) Japan
c) Saudi Arabia
d) Iran

15. **Often players are transferred from a club in one country to a club in another country. Between the clubs of which two countries do professional players move the most?**

a) From Austria to Germany
b) From Brazil to Portugal
c) From France to Belgium
d) From Togo to Ghana

16. **Match the flag to the World Cup host country. (The World Cup years are included for both the men's and women's competitions.)**

a) Australia 2023
b) Brazil 1950, 2014
c) Canada 2015
d) Qatar 2022
e) South Korea 2002
f) USA 1994, 1999, 2003

1)   2)   3)

4)   5)   6)

17. **FIFA ranks all national teams from best to worst based on results. The following teams have all been ranked in the top five at some point since 2000. Can you list them in order of population size, from largest to smallest?**

a) Argentina
b) Brazil
c) Croatia
d) England

e) Germany
f) Netherlands
g) Uruguay

18. **As football has grown in popularity around the world, so have football variants, such as futsal, a type of five-a-side football played indoors that favours fast, agile and technically gifted players. Brazil, Portugal, Spain and Italy all have professional futsal leagues. Compared to a normal football, a futsal ball is:**

a) Smaller and lighter
b) Smaller and heavier
c) Bigger and heavier
d) Bigger and lighter

19. **Every two years, FIFA organizes a five-a-side World Cup competition for teams that like to play by the sea. What's the competition called?**

a) Foot Volley World Cup
b) Beach Soccer World Cup
c) Stand-up Paddleboard World Cup
d) Underwater Football World Cup

20. **Bill Shankly, the charismatic Scottish coach of Liverpool in the 1960s, made one of the most famous comments about football:**

What's the missing word?

> Some people think football is a matter of life and death. I assure you, it's much more .... than that.

a) Funny
b) Smelly
c) Scary
d) Important

GUTSY GOALIES AND DOGGED DEFENDERS

Let's turn our attention to what happens on the pitch. Football is about scoring goals – but it is also about stopping them! In the long run, it is just as important to keep the ball out of your own net as it is to put it in your opponent's. To win matches you need goalscorers, but to win titles you need a good defence.

The job of keepers and defenders is to obstruct and prevent, as opposed to the job of forwards to dazzle and create. Yet we think there is great beauty and skill in the best defenders. Just as we can marvel at a wonder strike, we can be awed by a super save, a brilliant block or a well-timed tackle. In these questions we salute these sturdy soldiers who protect the goal at all costs.

A strong keeper is the foundation of all good sides. You need to be able to trust your keeper never to lose their calm or concentration. Keepers have the number 1 on their backs, which underlines their unique role: the only one to wear a different colour kit, to wear gloves and to be able to catch the ball. It's a lonely job!

Defenders, on the other hand, always act together. They play in unison, keeping in line, backing each other up and making sure no dangerous gaps emerge. If the defence is well positioned, attackers will find it hard to break though.

Diving saves! Slide tackles! Safe hands! You won't let this chapter slip through the net!

1. **Goalkeepers were an important part of football as soon as the game was invented, but their role on the pitch has changed slightly over time. Can you put the following goalkeeper-related rules in the order in which they were introduced?**

   a) Goalkeepers cannot pick up a back pass.
   b) Goalkeepers can only handle the ball in the penalty area.
   c) In a World Cup, goalkeeper gloves must be a different colour from the goalkeeper's jersey.
   d) Goalkeepers must keep at least one foot on the line when a penalty is struck.
   e) Goalkeepers must wear different colour jerseys from their team.
   f) Goalkeepers wear the number 1 on their jersey for international matches.

2. **Complete the following phrase which is used when a goalkeeper does not let in any goals in a game:**
   Keeping a clean ...

   a) ... net.
   b) ... goal.
   c) ... sheet.
   d) ... slate.

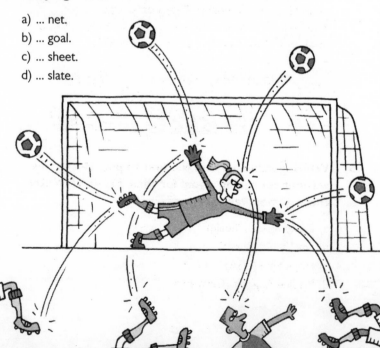

3. **Match these goalkeepers to the country they play for:**

GOALKEEPER	COUNTRY
a) Jan Oblak	1) Germany
b) Keylor Navas	2) Denmark
c) Christiane Endler	3) Belgium
d) Édouard Mendy	4) Spain
e) Ederson	5) USA
f) Marc André ter Stegen	6) Slovenia
g) Sandra Paños	7) Senegal
h) Kasper Schmeichel	8) Costa Rica
i) Thibaut Courtois	9) Chile
j) Alyssa Naeher	10) Brazil

4. **In one of the most heroic goalkeeping performances of all time, Manchester City goalkeeper Bert Trautmann broke a bone during the 1956 FA Cup final and played on. What did he break?**

a) Arm
b) Leg
c) Neck
d) Wrist

5. **Which goalkeeper was the first to play 100 games without conceding a goal for their country? (Note: these games were not consecutive!)**

a) David de Gea (Spain)
b) Lev Yashin (Russia)
c) Hope Solo (USA)
d) Nadine Angerer (Germany)

6. **Which country has the most goalkeepers who have captained their teams to winning the Men's World Cup?**

   a) Brazil
   b) Germany
   c) France
   d) Italy

7. **Goalkeepers usually exude calmness and solidity, but a few are famous for their eccentricities, such as the South American who (in a game against England) invented an outrageous type of goal-line clearance. The Scorpion Kick is an acrobatic dive in which the ball is heeled forward when the keeper is floating mid-air. What was his name?**

   a) José Luis Chilavert (Paraguay)
   b) René Higuita (Colombia)
   c) Claudio Bravo (Chile)
   d) Ederson (Brazil)

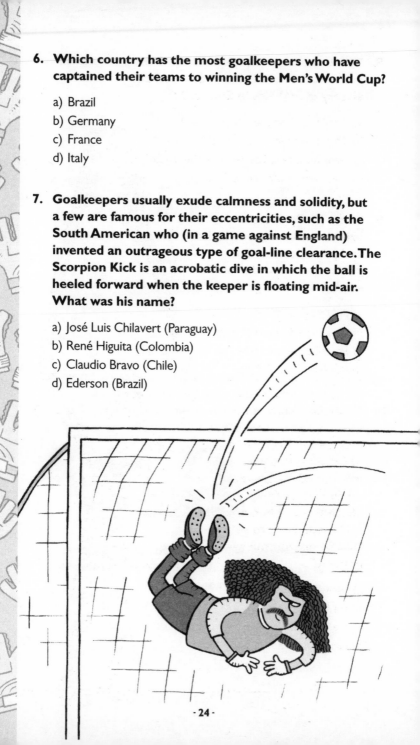

8. **What special connection did the Danish and Welsh goalkeepers have in Denmark's knockout round victory over Wales in Euro 2020?**

   a) They both had the same name.
   b) They played for the same club.
   c) They both saved penalties in the match.
   d) They were both sent off.

9. **Some goalkeepers are brilliant at taking free kicks and penalties. Put these goalkeepers in order of who scored the most goals.**

   a) Alisson (Brazil)
   b) José Luis Chilavert (Paraguay)
   c) Peter Schmeichel (Denmark)
   d) Rogério Ceni (Brazil)

10. **Gianluigi Donnarumma, the Italy goalkeeper who was named Player of the Tournament at Euro 2020, was tipped for greatness when he was only eight by his coach Ernesto Ferraro. What skill made Ferraro so sure that Donnarumma would make it?**

    a) He was a good listener.
    b) He had long arms.
    c) He had a loud voice.
    d) He was brave.

11. What award did USA defender Crystal Dunn win while playing for Washington Spirit in the top division of the American league, the NWSL, in 2015?

a) The Golden Boot for the most goals
b) The Red Boot for the most red cards
c) The Yellow Boot for the most yellow cards
d) The Green Boot for the most tackles

12. Dutch defender Virgil van Dijk has won the Premier League and Champions League with Liverpool. He made his professional debut at the relatively late age of 20. What was his job before then?

a) Trainee doctor
b) Fixing broken mobile phones
c) Writing speeches for a local politician
d) Washing dishes in a restaurant

13. **When a team is defending against a corner, there are generally two defence strategies. One is "man-marking", in which each player must mark a specific opponent and stick with them wherever they go. The other strategy is for each player to defend a specific space or area of the pitch. What's the second strategy called?**

    a) Spatial marking
    b) Aerial marking
    c) Zonal marking
    d) Specific marking

14. **What terrible fate befell Brazilian defender Thiago Silva, who won the 2021 Champions League with Chelsea, when he played for Russian side Dynamo Moscow as a teenager?**

    a) He ran over his dog which had been flown over from Brazil to make him feel less homesick.
    b) He contracted an illness, almost died and spent six months in the same room until he recovered.
    c) He scored an own goal in each of his first three appearances for the club.
    d) He was sick on the club owner's wife on the day he signed.

15. **Defenders are also known as "backs". There are full-backs, centre-backs and wing-backs. What is the main job of a wing-back?**

   a) To provide the team with width
   b) To push forward to help the attack
   c) To track back to help the defence
   d) All of the above

16. **Which former England defender, now a television presenter, scored the winning goal for Arsenal in their first-ever European trophy success, winning the UEFA Women's Cup in 2007?**

   a) Karen Carney
   b) Alex Scott
   c) Steph Houghton
   d) Rachel Brown-Finnis

17. **Which defender has won 44 trophies in his career, for both club and country, more than any other player?**

   a) Dani Alves (Brazil)
   b) Sergio Ramos (Spain)
   c) Kyle Walker (England)
   d) Giorgio Chiellini (Italy)

Who am I?

18. **A *libero* is the name given to a spare defender who plays behind the defence, offering another layer of security before the goalkeeper. It's an Italian word – what does it mean?**

   a) Free
   b) Extra
   c) Handsome
   d) Librarian

19. **What did Italy defender Leo Bonucci eat before a big game to put off his opponents after being told that in ancient times soldiers did the same thing?**

   a) Baked beans to fart at his opponents
   b) Cabbage, after which he had a bath in his own urine
   c) Garlic tablets to breathe on his opponents
   d) Durian, an Asian fruit that smells like rotten onions

20. **Christie Rampone is a former World Cup-winning defender who played over 300 matches for the USA women's national team. Complete her quote about the importance of defenders:**

   "If we score, we might win. If they never score ..."

   a) ... I will score instead.
   b) ... we can't lose.
   c) ... the crowd will fall asleep.
   d) ... they might lose.

WHAT'S IN A NAME?

What does every footballer want to make for themselves, but already has? A name! In this chapter we will take a proper look at the proper names throughout the game, from players to clubs and national teams. It's our calling!

We'll be travelling the world to discover curiously named clubs, and imaginatively nicknamed national teams. We'll also look at the original meanings of towns and cities with famous football clubs. Through names we can explore the history, geography and culture of sport.

In most countries, such as the UK, players are generally known by their surnames. In some countries, such as Brazil, players are known by their first names or nicknames. In Iceland, however, players are known by the names of their parents! For example, the midfielder Aron Gunnarsson is Icelandic for Aron, son of Gunnar. Nice one, son!

Let's begin our roll call. Name tags on!

1. **Can you match the first part of these British club names to the second?**

a)	Accrington	1)	Academical
b)	Bolton	2)	Albion
c)	Brighton & Hove	3)	Argyle
d)	Cambridge	4)	Athletic
e)	Charlton	5)	City
f)	Derby	6)	County
g)	Hamilton	7)	Orient
h)	Huddersfield	8)	Rangers
i)	Leyton	9)	Stanley
j)	Partick	10)	Thistle
k)	Plymouth	11)	Town
l)	Queens Park	12)	United
m)	Swansea	13)	Wanderers

2. **How did Sheffield Wednesday get its name?**

a) Wednesday is an area in Sheffield.
b) The club started as a cricket club that played their games on Wednesdays.
c) The founder was the football pioneer Wilberforce Wednesday.
d) The founders couldn't think of a name and so opened a dictionary at a random page.

3. Match the nicknames to the British clubs:

a) Barnsley
b) Brentford
c) Bristol City
d) Heart of Midlothian
e) Newcastle United
f) Peterborough
g) Reading
h) Southampton
i) Southend United
j) Sunderland

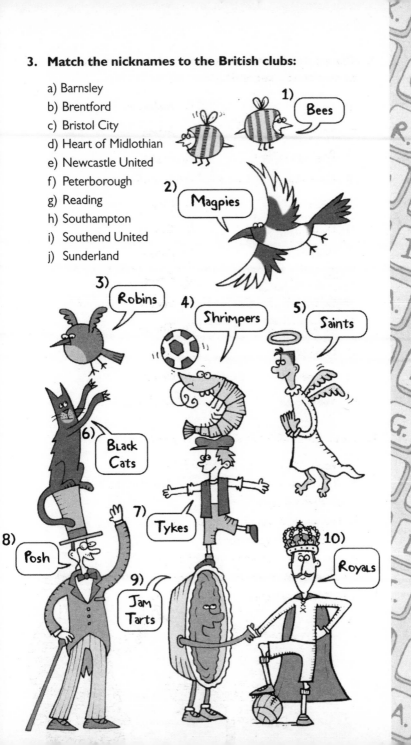

4. **Complete the following sentence: Hull City is the only professional club in England whose name ...**

   a) ... does not contain any of the letters A, B, D, E, G, O, P, Q, which are the only letters that contain a closed loop.
   (This means it is the only club that does not have letters that have a part that can be coloured in.)

   b) ... contains a word that originates from Old Norse.

   c) ... is two words of exactly four letters.

   d) ... is made up of two words, the first having one syllable and the second having two syllables.

5. **Many clubs are named after the cities or towns in which they are based. But some famous clubs have more colourful names. Can you match these fixtures to the countries where they are played?**

MATCH		COUNTRY
a) Orlando Pirates v. Kaizer Chiefs	1)	Bolivia
b) Young Boys v. Grasshoppers	2)	Chile
c) The Strongest v. Always Ready	3)	Egypt
d) Odd v. Viking	4)	Ghana
e) Hearts of Oak v. Eleven Wonders	5)	Greece
f) National Bank v. Pyramids	6)	Norway
g) Lokomotiv v. Torpedo	7)	Russia
h) OL Reign v. Angel City	8)	South Africa
i) Olympiacos v. Panathinaikos	9)	Switzerland
j) Colo-Colo v. O'Higgins	10)	USA

6. **"Doing the Poznań" is a way of celebrating goals popularized in England by fans of Manchester City. The name derives from the Polish side Lech Poznań, whose fans performed the celebration when City played them in the Europa Cup in 2010. What did they do?**

   a) Every fan waved an inflatable banana in the air.
   b) Every fan grabbed the arm of the person next to them and danced the polka.
   c) Fans took off all their clothes and jumped up and down.
   d) The fans turned their backs to the pitch, joined arms, jumped up and down and started to sing.

7. **Sometimes countries change their names due to having new borders or new political systems. Which of the following four countries is the only one that has always sent a national team to the World Cup with the same name?**

   a) Czech Republic
   b) Germany
   c) Ukraine
   d) Hungary

8. Can you match the following fixtures featuring the nicknames of international teams to the proper names of the countries they represent?

FIXTURE

a) The Brave Gentlemen v. The Samurai Blue

b) The Squirrels v. The Crocodiles

c) The Reggae Girlz v. The Black Queens

d) The War Elephants v. The Grasshoppers

e) The Owls v. The Eagles

f) The Dragons v. The Dragons

g) The Dodos v. The Cranes

h) The Snow Leopards v. The Three Lions

i) The Street Dogs v. The Lions of Mesopotamia

j) The Matildas v. The Canaries

COUNTRY

1) Benin v. Lesotho

2) Jordan v. Japan

3) Thailand women v. Norway women

4) Jamaica women v. Ghana women

5) Philippines v. Iraq

6) Mauritius v. Uganda

7) Wales v. Slovenia

8) Australia women v. Brazil women

9) Finland v. Serbia

10) Kazakhstan v. England

9. Each continent has its own football confederation,
    which governs the sport in that continent. **UEFA** is the
    confederation for Europe, and **CONCACAF** represents
    North America. What is the name of the South
    American confederation, which is an abbreviation of
    Confederación Sudamericana de Fútbol?

    a) CONFESUD
    b) CONMEFUT
    c) CONMEBOL
    d) CONSUFU

10. **Scottish club Aberdeen play at Pittodrie Stadium.
    What does *pittodrie* mean in Gaelic?**

    a) House of pleasure
    b) Land of gold
    c) Hill of dung
    d) Pit of despair

11. **Which of the following players represents the same
    country as her name?**

    a) Jenny Wales
    b) Bethany England
    c) Francine France
    d) Erin Scotland

12. **After which famous person was Cristiano Ronaldo named?**

   a) Ronald McDonald, the mascot of the fast-food chain
   b) Ronald Weasley, the character in the Harry Potter books
   c) Ronald O'Sullivan, the snooker player
   d) Ronald Reagan, the US president

13. **Former Juventus and Brazil midfielder Filipe Melo named his son after an England forward, but changed the spelling. What is his son's name?**

   a) Linyker
   b) Rooni
   c) Harricaine
   d) She-Rah

14. **What is the middle name of England defender Lucy Bronze?**

   a) Tough
   b) Rusty
   c) Brilliant
   d) Copper

15. **Which famous team was called Newton Heath when it was founded in 1878, only changing its name in 1902 to what it is called today?**

a) Arsenal
b) Liverpool
c) Manchester United
d) Newcastle United

16. **The England team has in recent years included players called Harry, Jordan, Raheem, Bukayo and Jude. These names come from different languages. Can you match the names to their original meanings?**

NAME	MEANING AND LANGUAGE
a) Bukayo	1) Adds to happiness (Yorùbá)
b) Jordan	2) Compassionate (Arabic)
c) Jude	3) Home ruler (Old German)
d) Raheem	4) Praise (Hebrew)
e) Harry	5) To go down (Hebrew)

17. **Often, Brazilian players have the Portuguese suffix "*inho*" added at the end of their names. For example, the footballers Fabinho, Marquinhos and Ronaldinho were actually born Fabio, Marcos and Ronaldo. What does "*inho*" mean?**

   a) Small
   b) Big
   c) Skilful
   d) Strong

18. **Cuauhtémoc Blanco, one of Mexico's greatest ever players, made a remarkable move in the 1998 World Cup which became known as the Cuauhtemiña. What did he do?**

   a) He picked up the ball between his heels and bunny-hopped over the legs of two defenders.
   b) He chipped the ball up, caught it on the back of his neck and, without it falling, ran past two players.
   c) He kicked the ball with so much spin that it flew about 50 yards, circled in the air and came back to him.
   d) He did a somersault in the air, landing in a handstand, in order to kick a high ball.

19. **What links the footballers Bernardo Silva of Portugal, Nigel de Jong of the Netherlands, Thomas Müller of Germany, Kelly Smith of England, Jonna Andersson of Sweden and Paolo Rossi of Italy?**

a) Their surnames all have the same meaning in their national languages.

b) They all changed their surnames when they professionalized, because their birth surnames were embarrassing (Bernardo Saliva, Nigel de Pong, Thomas Muppet, Kelly Snot, Jonna Sillyson and Paulo Spaghetti).

c) They each have the most common surname in their native country.

d) Their surnames all derive from words in their languages for manual jobs.

20. **Match the names of the following footballers with the meanings of the surnames in their languages:**

NAME	MEANING
a) Jordi Alba (Spain)	1) Fox
b) Ciro Immobile (Italy)	2) Goat
c) Teemu Pukki (Finland)	3) Motionless
d) Wendie Renard (France)	4) Sunrise

BALLS AND BOWLS

This chapter is all about the balls that players kick and the bowls they kick in. In other words, it's about the basic equipment you need to play football: an air-filled, leather sphere and a fan-filled stadium!

Modern stadiums are giant bowls – that's the architectural term. The seats are lined up around the sides of the bowl and the pitch is at the bottom. The bowl is designed so as many people as possible have a good view.

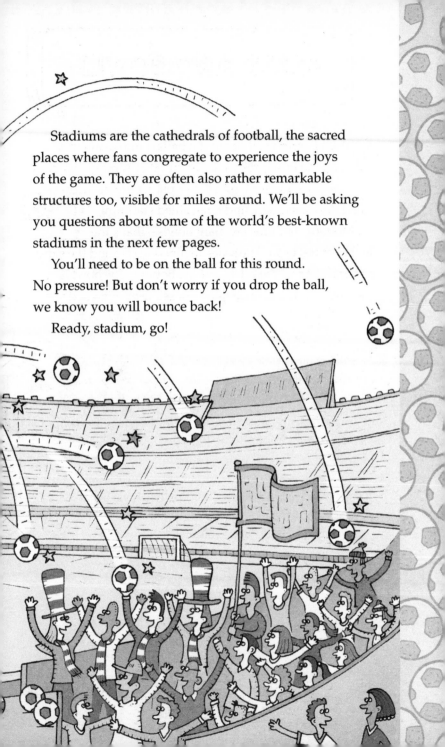

Stadiums are the cathedrals of football, the sacred places where fans congregate to experience the joys of the game. They are often also rather remarkable structures too, visible for miles around. We'll be asking you questions about some of the world's best-known stadiums in the next few pages.

You'll need to be on the ball for this round. No pressure! But don't worry if you drop the ball, we know you will bounce back!

Ready, stadium, go!

1. What were the earliest British footballs made from?

   a) Sheep's brains
   b) Cows' buttocks
   c) Pigs' bladders
   d) Whales' testicles

2. FIFA requires that professional balls pass several performance tests. What is the official test to make sure that balls retain their size, shape and pressure?

   a) A professional "kicker" employed by the factory is given 10 minutes to kick a ball against a wall.
   b) A car is driven over the ball ten times.
   c) The ball is put in a freezer for 24 hours, then soaked in water for 24 hours, then dropped 1,000 times from a height of 2m onto a steel plate.
   d) A machine fires the ball 2,000 times at a steel plate at 50km per hour.

3. **The classic football (illustrated below) is based on a geometrical object called a "truncated icosahedron", in which 32 flat shapes are stitched together. Which ones are they?**

a) 3 pentagons and 29 hexagons
b) 12 pentagons and 20 hexagons
c) 24 pentagons and 8 hexagons
d) 4 triangles, 6 squares, 10 pentagons and 12 hexagons

4. **Manufacturers love to give their balls jazzy names before each tournament. Which five names below are of balls that have been used at a World Cup?**

a) Spheria
b) Betelgeuse
c) Tango
d) Brazuca
e) Telstar
f) Goldenball
g) Jabulani
h) Spinderella
i) Azteca
j) Samba

5. **The science behind ball design improves every year. The Premier League ball used in the 2021–22 season includes three of the four following technologies. Which one did we make up?**

a) Smart Lightweight Intelligence Processing (SLIP) technology that uses an internal computer to stop players slipping when they kick the ball.

b) All Conditions Control (ACC) technology, which means you get the same grip in the wet and in the dry.

c) 3D-printed ink that adds texture to the ball that helps with aerodynamic performance.

d) AerowSculpt technology, which creates grooves around the ball to reduce wobble when it moves through the air.

6. **In winter months, Premier League balls are different from the balls used at the beginning of the season. How?**

a) They are made with an inner lining of wool, because of the cold.

b) They are made of a less absorbent material, because winter is usually wetter than the other seasons.

c) They have a thin film of anti-freeze around them, just in case it snows.

d) They are a high-vis yellow, because there is less light in the winter.

7. **Which city has for years been the world's biggest producer of stitched leather footballs, fabricating tens of millions of balls every year?**

   a) Ballymena, Ireland
   b) Shenzhen, China
   c) Sialkot, Pakistan
   d) Palermo, Italy

8. **The word "stadium" comes from the Greek "*stadion*", meaning what?**

   a) A large, ornate bowl
   b) A field of grass
   c) A stage
   d) An ancient unit of measurement, corresponding to the length of a running track

9. **The first stadium built specifically for football opened in 1892. Which stadium was it?**

   a) Goodison Park (Everton)
   b) Bramall Lane (Sheffield United)
   c) Stamford Bridge (Chelsea)
   d) Celtic Park (Celtic)

10. **The highest attendance ever for a football match is thought to have been the final of the 1950 World Cup at the Maracanã in Rio de Janeiro, at which almost 200,000 people watched Uruguay beat Brazil 2–1. Attendances are much lower now at big stadiums because they have seats (rather than standing room), which take up space. What is currently the world's largest stadium that is used for football matches, with a capacity of around 114,000?**

   a) Camp Nou, Barcelona
   b) Wembley, London
   c) Rungrado 1st of May, Pyongyang, North Korea
   d) Maracanã, Rio de Janeiro

11. **What part of the stadium is known as the vomitory?**

   a) A small cubicle next to the dressing room where nervous players can be sick before a game
   b) An area behind the coach's dugout where injured players can be treated
   c) The coach's office, so called because England's first-ever coach Walter Winterbottom used to be sick before matches
   d) The corridors that fans walk through when they enter or leave the stadium

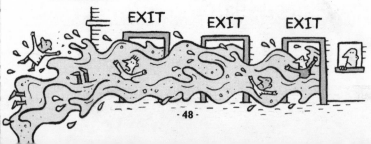

12. Match the stadiums to the football clubs:

STADIUM	CLUB
a) Allianz Arena	1) Real Madrid
b) Anfield	2) AC Milan
c) La Bombonera	3) Ajax
d) Estadio Azteca	4) Paris Saint-Germain
e) Johan Cruyff Stadium	5) Liverpool
f) Old Trafford	6) Bayern Munich
g) Parc des Princes	7) Boca Juniors
h) San Siro	8) Borussia Dortmund
i) Santiago Bernabéu	9) Club América
j) Westfalenstadion	10) Manchester United

13. All of these football heroes have a stadium named after them, except one. Which one?

a) Vero Boquete
b) Didier Drogba
c) Cristiano Ronaldo
d) Diego Maradona

14. Match the following characteristics to the correct stadiums:

CHARACTERISTIC

a) The football pitch splits into three sections and can be moved underneath the stands, revealing an American football pitch below.

b) There are no seats behind one goal; instead there is a giant rock-face.

c) It is the highest national stadium in the world, located at 3,637 metres above sea level.

d) In 2011 it held the world record for the loudest crowd roar at a sports stadium (the record now belongs to an American football stadium in the US).

STADIUM

1) Braga Stadium, Portugal

2) Estadio Hernando Siles, Bolivia

3) Tottenham Hotspur Stadium, England

4) Türk Telekom Stadium, Turkey

15. Which fact below about the Zerão (Big Zero) stadium in the Brazilian Amazon is true?

a) Anaconda snakes are placed in a small moat around much of the pitch to stop pitch invasions.

b) The equator runs across the halfway line, so each half is in a different hemisphere.

c) It is the only professional pitch in the world where the pitch is made up entirely of mud, because of the difficulty of maintaining grass in the rainforest.

d) It's where Alex proposed to his wife.

16. What is the only stadium of a professional English team that's on an island?

a) Fratton Park (Portsmouth)
b) Craven Cottage (Fulham)
c) Sincil Bank (Lincoln)
d) Blundell Park (Grimsby Town)

17. Manchester City were the first Premier League team to launch a Tunnel Club for its fans. What do fans who are in the Tunnel Club get to do?

a) Watch the players in the tunnel before they go out onto the pitch
b) Watch the players training during the week from a tunnel next to the training ground
c) Give the players a high-five at half-time as they walk through the tunnel
d) Listen to the coach's team-talks from the tunnel

18. **Wembley is the England team's national stadium. It was first used in 1923, and built with two iconic towers measuring 126 feet high, known as the Twin Towers. The stadium was rebuilt in 2000 and re-opened in 2003 with a new iconic landmark that could be seen for miles (including by England striker Raheem Sterling from his childhood home). What was it?**

a) A giant W
b) A giant sculpture of a lion
c) A giant arch
d) A giant laser

19. **Turkish club Bursaspor have built their stadium in the shape of the club's animal mascot. What's the stadium called?**

a) Turtle Dome
b) Snake Stadium
c) Crocodile Arena
d) Iguana World

20. Forest Green Rovers is the greenest club in football: it generates its own solar energy, plays on an organic pitch and irrigates the turf using rainwater. How will its new stadium, Eco Park, make the club even greener?

a) Everything in the stadium will be painted totally green, and the dress code (for everyone except opposing fans) will be green.

b) The car park will only allow electric cars.

c) It will be built almost entirely from wood, a renewable building material.

d) The toilets will be compost loos, where there is no flush: you just poo or wee on a pile of sawdust.

MARVELLOUS MIDFIELDERS AND STAR STRIKERS

The aim of every football team is to score goals and, in most teams, the players whose job it is to do that are those in midfield and attack. The midfield is the creative hub, where playmakers find ways to get the ball through opposition defences. They aim to get the ball to the strikers or centre-forwards, the goal-machines with a killer instinct for finding the back of the net. Or sometimes the midfielders will score themselves. That's what makes football exciting and unpredictable – there are many, many ways to score; every team, and every player, does it differently.

Fans always want to see their forwards on the ball, because every attack contains at least a glimmer of a chance of a goal. These are the players that get the biggest cheers, and whose skills – the dribbles, the passes, the shots on goal – are the most thrilling to watch. The goalscorer is always the hero, and since the goalscorers are usually forwards, these players are usually the most idolized by fans. It's not surprising that the most famous players in the history of the game – from Maradona to Messi, Marta to Miedema – all played in attack.

In this chapter, we will set up the chances for you by asking some questions about these players – you just need to finish them off with the right answers. Pass, chance, goooaaall!

1. **Can you match these World Cup-winning midfielders to the countries they played for?**

   MIDFIELDER

   a) Sir Bobby Charlton
   b) Andrés Iniesta
   c) Toni Kroos
   d) Rose Lavelle
   e) Diego Maradona
   f) Ronaldinho
   g) Andrea Pirlo
   h) Paul Pogba
   i) Homare Sawa

   COUNTRY

   1) Argentina
   2) Brazil
   3) England
   4) France
   5) Germany
   6) Italy
   7) Japan
   8) Spain
   9) USA

2. **England midfielder Declan Rice plays for the national team alongside another midfielder who is also his best friend. The pair have been besties since they played in the same team aged eight. Who is his friend?**

   a) Jadon Sancho
   b) Kalvin Phillips
   c) Mason Mount
   d) Ben White

3. **The midfield is a large space, and different types of midfielder take on different roles. The shirt number often denotes the type of player. Below are five midfield roles and the five shirt numbers most commonly associated with them. Can you match the positions to the numbers?**

   a) Attacking midfielder: creating opportunities for the strikers
   b) Ball-winning midfielder: stays in own half to tackle opponents and start attacks
   c) Box-to-box midfielder: running in between each penalty area, often scoring too
   d) Holding midfielder: sits in front of the defence to win possession
   e) Wide midfielder: dribbles and crosses from the wing

4. **Zinedine Zidane of France was the best midfielder in the world at the beginning of the 21st century. The final match of his career was the 2006 World Cup final against Italy. The game started well for him with a chipped penalty in the first half. But what memorable incident happened after that?**

   a) He scored two own goals and France lost 2–1.
   b) He vomited on the referee.
   c) He headbutted an opponent and was sent off.
   d) He missed the crucial penalty in the shoot-out, which France lost.

5. **Lionel Messi has won the Ballon D'Or more times than anyone else, and holds the record (50) for the most official goals scored in a league season. Which of the following statements is the best description of his style of play?**

a) He typically runs more than other forwards, tiring out defenders.

b) He typically spends most of his time dribbling, so he keeps making chances.

c) He typically runs much less than other forwards, instead walking and looking for space to run into.

d) He typically talks more than other players, telling team-mates where to position themselves.

6. **Cristiano Ronaldo has scored over 100 goals by heading the ball into the net, and is widely considered to be one of the best headers of the ball in football history. He can jump over 75cm to head the ball, which is higher than the average leaping height in what sport?**

a) High jump

b) Pole vault

c) Ski jumping

d) Basketball

7. **Marco Verratti played in Italy's midfield when they won Euro 2020. Why was his achievement significant?**

   a) He was 27 and had never played a single match in Serie A, Italy's top division.
   b) Instead of holding hands with a mascot before the game, he entered the pitch with his grandma.
   c) He completed every one of his 124 passes in the final against England.
   d) He dyed his hair the colours of the Italian flag for the final.

8. **How did Norway winger Caroline Graham Hansen impress TV viewers who challenged her on a game show?**

   a) She memorized a 120-line poem in one hour.
   b) She beat chess grandmaster Magnus Carlsen.
   c) She balanced a football on her head for ten minutes while being interviewed.
   d) She juggled a ball with her feet from the bottom floor of an office block to a rooftop terrace several storeys up – without it touching the ground once.

9. **Which five of these great strikers have won the World Cup?**

   a) Kylian Mbappé
   b) Lionel Messi
   c) Robert Lewandowski
   d) Thomas Müller
   e) Cristiano Ronaldo
   f) Antoine Griezmann
   g) Romelu Lukaku
   h) Harry Kane
   i) Vivianne Miedema
   j) Alex Morgan
   k) Sam Kerr
   l) Pernille Harder
   m) Megan Rapinoe

10. **Pelé won three World Cups playing for Brazil – in 1958, 1970 and 1974. When he retired, he spent much of his time travelling the world as a businessman and celebrity. What one item from his childhood did he always bring on his trips to remind him of home?**

   a) His first-ever football
   b) A pot of sand from his local beach
   c) A fluffy teddy bear
   d) A wooden spinning top

11. **Alfredo Di Stéfano was the striker whose goals helped Real Madrid win the first five editions of the European Cup, the forerunner to the Champions League. What is his claim to fame in international football?**

a) He scored a hat-trick of hat-tricks: three goals in each of his first three games for Argentina.

b) He played for three different countries: Argentina, Colombia and Spain.

c) He won the World Cup playing for Uruguay and did the same four years later playing for Italy.

d) He was the first player to win the World Cup as a player and then a coach.

12. **How does Kylian Mbappé describe his playing style?**

a) Speed, skill, goals – and a smart haircut

b) The modern attacker who can play anywhere

c) Pass and move, always with the aim to score

d) My job is to win the game first and entertain the fans second

13. **England midfielder Kalvin Phillips wore a shirt with the name of his hero on the back of it to celebrate England reaching the Euro 2020 final. What was the name?**

   a) Lewis Hamilton
   b) Alex Bellos
   c) The Queen
   d) Granny Val

14. **Australia striker Sam Kerr could have represented three other countries based on where her grandparents came from. Which ones?**

   a) New Zealand, USA, Croatia
   b) Scotland, Wales, Pakistan
   c) Tonga, Spain, China
   d) England, Ireland, India

15. There are many different ways to describe how a striker plays. Which five of the following are real terms used to describe how certain strikers play?

a) Goal poacher

b) Shoulder runner

c) Deep sprinter

d) Fox in the box

e) Cheeky devil

f) False nine

g) Second striker

h) Inverted classic

i) Mobile shadow

j) Pressing forward

16. Which midfielder won the 2021 Ballon D'Or for the world's best player after helping Barcelona Femení win the Spanish league, the Spanish Cup and the Champions League?

a) Irene Paredes

b) Aitana Bonmatí

c) Alexia Putellas

d) Lieke Martens

17. **Christine Sinclair scored more international goals than any other player when she scored number 185 for Canada in 2020. One year later she won her first international trophy with her national team. What was it?**

   a) The Olympic Games
   b) The World Cup
   c) The Gold Cup
   d) The Confederations Cup

18. **Only a handful of players have managed to score 100 goals or more for their international teams. Which five of the players below have managed this feat?**

   a) Cristiano Ronaldo (Portugal)
   b) Zlatan Ibrahimović (Sweden)
   c) Pelé (Brazil)
   d) Ali Daei (Iran)
   e) Ferenc Puskás (Hungary)
   f) Birgit Prinz (Germany)
   g) Marta (Brazil)
   h) Kelly Smith (England)
   i) Abby Wambach (USA)
   j) Jenni Hermoso (Spain)

19. **In what city was Norway striker Erling Haaland born? (At the time his dad, Alf-Inge Haaland, was playing in the Premier League.)**

   a) Nottingham
   b) Manchester
   c) Leeds
   d) Molde

20. **Which Belgium striker played at Euro 2020 in the national team alongside his younger brother (who scored twice)?**

   a) Romelu Lukaku
   b) Christian Benteke
   c) Dries Mertens
   d) Eden Hazard

TROPHIES AND TOURNAMENTS

What do teams want? Trophies! When do they want them? At the end of the season!

Anyone who follows football needs to know about the competitions that give structure to the calendar. Clubs and national teams can play in different leagues and cups. In fact, a player at a top English club may get to play in six club competitions: the Premier League, the FA Cup, the League Cup, the Champions League, the Europa League and the Club World Cup. National teams get to play in their continental championships and in the World Cup – at least in the qualifying stages! A few countries even send teams to the Olympics. A profusion of prizes! A cornucopia of cups!

All competitions have a trophy, a physical object given to the winning team in order to commemorate the victory. Trophies are important for players and fans to remind them of glorious results. That's why cups get collected in trophy cabinets and not thrown in the bin! In this chapter we'll be testing your knowledge on cups and competitions in Europe and across the world.

Do you know your trophies, or will we sur-prize you? These questions will medal with your mind!

1. **Here are five famous football trophies, can you tell us what they are?**

a)   b)   c)

d)   e)

2. **Sometimes trophy celebrations go wrong. Three of the four following events actually happened. Which one did we make up?**

a) When Real Madrid won the 2011 Copa del Rey, the team paraded the trophy on an open-top bus. Defender Sergio Ramos accidentally dropped the trophy from the top deck and the bus ran it over.

b) On winning the 2012 Dutch league title with Ajax, Jan Vertonghen dropped the trophy on his toe. He had already taken his boots off and the blood could be seen through his socks. Ouch!

c) When Paris Saint-Germain won the French league in 2020, Neymar put his head in the trophy for a laugh and for a few minutes his head got stuck.

d) When Corinthians won the 2009 São Paulo state championship in Brazil, a firework accidentally lit a volley of paper streamers that had been fired in the air above the cup. As a result, the cup caught fire.

3. The World Cup trophy is mostly made of gold, is 36.8cm high (about the length of a cucumber) and weighs 6.1kg. The weight of the trophy is roughly equal to how many copies of this book?

a) 5
b) 10
c) 20
d) 35

4. Sometimes, trophies are given to individual players. For example, the Golden Boot is given to the top-scorer at a World Cup, and the Golden Ball to the best player. Who is the most recent player to have won both the Golden Boot and the Golden Ball at the same World Cup?

a) Cristiano Ronaldo
b) Harry Kane
c) Megan Rapinoe
d) Pelé

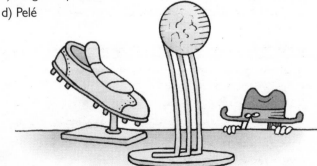

5. **The Henri Delaunay Cup is the name given to the trophy awarded at the European Championship (the Euros). Delaunay was a Frenchman who was one of the founders of the competition. He was also a referee who retired after a strange but horrific accident. What was it?**

a) He swallowed the whistle and lost two teeth when a ball hit him in the face.

b) He ran into the goal post and broke his nose and jaw.

c) He flipped the coin at the beginning of the match and it lodged so far up his nose that he lost his sense of smell.

d) He lost an eye when, on trying to break up a fight between two players, he was punched in the face by both of them.

6. **Match the league name to the country:**

LEAGUE NAME	COUNTRY
a) Allsvenskan	1) Australia
b) Bundesliga	2) England and Wales
c) Ekstraklasa	3) France
d) Eredivisie	4) Germany
e) J.League	5) Italy
f) La Liga	6) Japan
g) Ligue 1	7) Netherlands
h) Major League Soccer	8) Poland
i) Premier League	9) Spain
j) Serie A	10) Sweden
k) A-League	11) USA

7. **In the Premier League, if the season ends with two teams tied at the top of the table with the same number of points, the winner is decided by which team has a better goal difference. In Spain, on the other hand, if the season ends with two teams tied at the top of the table, the winner is the team ...**

a) ... that conceded the fewest goals.

b) ... that scored the most goals.

c) ... that has the better record in matches between the tied teams.

d) ... that wins a play-off match between the tied teams.

8. **What is the name of the top division in England in the women's game?**

a) W-League

b) Women's Super League

c) Women's Premier League

d) Women's Stars League

9. **What happened in the 1946 and 1947 FA Cup finals but has never happened since?**

a) Two second-division teams won the final.

b) Both captains were sent off.

c) The ball burst.

d) A dog ran on the pitch.

10. **What is unique about the Coupe de France, the French knockout tournament that is their equivalent of the FA Cup?**

a) Penalty shoot-outs are not allowed, so games that are tied after 90 minutes must continue until there is a goal. The longest game, between Paris Saint-Germain and Monaco in 1976, lasted for 25 hours.

b) A handicap system is used. If the two teams playing each other come from different tiers, the team in the lower tier is given a number of goals equal to the difference in tiers between the two teams. So if a Ligue 1 side is playing a Ligue 3 side, the game starts 2–0 for the Ligue 3 side.

c) Every team that enters must also enter a local cheese in a parallel competition for the best cheese in France. If a club gets knocked out, but their cheese has reached the quarter-finals, the team gets reinstated.

d) Clubs based in French overseas territories – such as Tahiti and New Caledonia in the Pacific, Réunion in the Indian Ocean, Guadeloupe in the Caribbean, and French Guiana in South America – are allowed to take part, which means that clubs often have to travel thousands of miles across the world to play games.

11. What is a round robin?

a) A knockout tournament

b) A tournament in which every team plays every other team

c) A tournament with a group stage and a knockout stage

d) A tournament where every fixture depends on the result of previous fixtures

12. The Champions League has its own anthem, which is played at the beginning of every Champions League match. It is based on a famous piece of classical music by which 18th-century composer?

a) Ludwig van Beethoven

b) George Frideric Handel

c) Jürgen Klopp

d) Wolfgang Amadeus Mozart

13. The African and Asian versions of the Champions League are called the African Champions League and the Asian Champions League. What's the South American version called?

a) The Real Champions League

b) The Copa Sudamericana

c) The Copa Libertadores

d) The Liga de los Campeones

14. Every year, FIFA hosts the Club World Cup, a competition played out between the winners of each continent's Champions League or equivalent competition. One other team gets to join this elite group – which is it?

a) The country that the player who won that year's FIFA's Best Player of the Year award plays for
b) A team chosen at random by the FIFA president
c) The league champions of the country where the game is played
d) The team that raised the most money for charitable causes that year

15. What is the oldest international football competition in the world that is still running?

a) The World Cup
b) The Copa América
c) The Asian Cup
d) The Euros

16. What did FIFA call the first-ever Women's World Cup in 1991?

a) FIFA Women's World Cup
b) 1st FIFA World Championship for Women's Football for the M&M's Cup
c) FIFA Football for Women Open World Competition
d) World Title for FIFA Women Footballers for the Mars Trophy

17. In what year was Euro 2020 held?

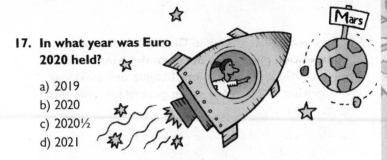

a) 2019
b) 2020
c) 2020½
d) 2021

18. The UEFA Nations League was first played in 2019 and won by Portugal. It usually takes place every two years, between a World Cup or European Championships. What reason did UEFA give for introducing the tournament?

a) A chance for Cristiano Ronaldo to win another trophy
b) So the 55 European countries could play fewer friendly matches and more competitive games
c) So UEFA could make more money from sponsors to put into the development of the game
d) So fans of small countries unlikely to qualify for the Euros or the World Cup can enjoy being in a competition

19. Which two teams won the football men's and women's gold medals in the 2020 Olympic Games?

a) Brazil and Canada
b) Spain and Sweden
c) Mexico and USA
d) Japan and Great Britain

20. Which one of the following statements about the FA Cup is true?

a) The FA Cup is the oldest football competition in the world.
b) The first FA Cup final was held at a rugby stadium.
c) No team has ever won the FA Cup and been relegated in the same season.
d) No player has ever been sent off in the FA Cup final.

SUPER STATS

Football is a numbers game. You need to be able to count to keep score, and also to read the league tables, check goal difference, tot up appearances, keep an eye on shirt numbers, study the top-scorers charts, and calculate your team's transfer spending. That's all part of the equation when it comes to the maths of football!

Numbers that are used to measure things – such as games played, goals scored, penalties missed, toes bruised and celebrations danced – are called statistics, or "stats". We need these numbers in order to work out who are football's record breakers, and we have included questions on some of our favourite record breakers below.

Statisticians – that's the people who work with statistics – love football as there are so many different ways to track the game. Nowadays, top teams measure all aspects of players' performance – from successful pass percentage to the speed of their sprints! Quick quick!

This chapter celebrates the numbers, the record breakers and the specialists who are counting more than just the scoreline. Are you ready to do a number on these questions? Three, two, one...

1. **Many clubs employ data analysts whose job is to analyse, or study, data. But what is data?**

   a) Strategy
   b) Meetings
   c) Facts about dates
   d) Any type of information expressed in numbers

2. **What was special about Burnley's starting lineup when they faced Liverpool in a Premier League match in August 2021. It was the first time this had happened in the Premier League in the 21st century. The 11 members of the starting line-up had ...**

   a) ... the squad numbers from 1 to 11.
   b) ... surnames beginning with the first 11 letters of the alphabet, from A to K.
   c) ... the squad numbers that were the first 11 even numbers, from 2 to 22.
   d) ... played in the World Cup for 11 different countries.

3. **In 2021, Cristiano Ronaldo broke the record for the most international goals scored by a male player when he reached 111 goals. Can you match the percentage of goals in the pie chart to the manner in which they were scored?**

   a) Right foot
   b) Left foot
   c) Header

   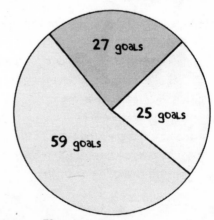

4. When French midfielder N'Golo Kanté helped Chelsea win the Premier League in 2017, he made history as what?

a) The first player to play every minute of the campaign without getting a yellow card
b) The first player to win the Premier League with two different clubs in two consecutive seasons
c) The first player to win the Premier League with the letters G, O, A and I in his name
d) The youngest player to win the Premier League

5. At the time of publication of this book, no male player has reached 200 international appearances. But more than 20 women have surpassed that total, including the most capped international ever, Kristine Lilly of the USA. How many international appearances did she make?

a) 224
b) 299
c) 354
d) 402

6. As of spring 2022, what record does Scottish side Rangers hold?

a) It has won the most titles of its domestic league in the world.
b) It has stayed in the top tier of its domestic league the longest without relegation.
c) It is the oldest club in the world still playing in its domestic league's top tier.
d) It changes its kit every 100 years – the next change is due in 2072.

7. **Sometimes, coaches will use a "heat map" to help them with tactics. What type of heat map is most commonly used in football?**

   a) A map of the pitch that shows its temperature at every point
   b) A map of a player's anatomy that shows variations in body temperature
   c) A map of the pitch that shows a particular player's location over the game: the places where the player spends most time are a different colour from the places the player hardly visits
   d) A clipboard that emits heat used by coaches during cold days

8. **Which is the only city to produce the teams that won the Champions League and Europa League trophies in the same season (clue: it happened in 2018)?**

   a) London
   b) Madrid
   c) Milan
   d) Munich

9. **Match the continent to the number of FIFA-accredited national teams in that continent.**

   a) Africa
   b) Asia
   c) Europe
   d) North America
   e) Oceania
   f) South America

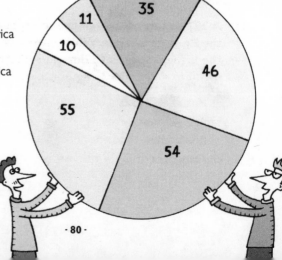

10. **Match the continent to the number of places at the 2022 World Cup given to that continent. (Four of the totals end in .5. This doesn't mean they have half a place! It means that these continents submitted a team in a play-off for the remaining two places. The host nation Qatar is not included.)**

a) Africa
b) Asia
c) Europe
d) North America
e) Oceania
f) South America

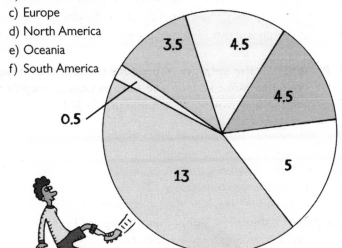

11. **A 2021 study measured the top speeds of players in the Premier League. Which player was fastest, reaching the highest speed of 32km per hour during a sprint in a Premier League game?**

a) Marcus Rashford
b) Adama Traoré
c) Kyle Walker
d) Andy Robertson

12. **Jack Grealish became the first British £100 million player when he transferred from Aston Villa to Manchester City for the 2021–22 season. If Manchester City had instead spent all the money on copies of this book (sold at £6.99) and stacked them one on top of the other, how high would the stack be?**

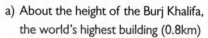

   a) About the height of the Burj Khalifa, the world's highest building (0.8km)
   b) About the height of Mount Everest, the world's highest mountain (9km)
   c) About the height of the highest ever flight in a jet plane (38km)
   d) About the height of a very low-orbiting satellite (200km)

13. **English goalkeeper Tom King entered the *Guinness World Records* in January 2021 for a very special kick he made for his team Newport County. What record did he achieve?**

   a) The longest goal ever scored in a competitive match (meaning the ball covered the longest distance before reaching the goal). He kicked the ball from his own box and it travelled 96.01m into the opposing net.
   b) The highest goal kick ever kicked in a competitive match, reaching an incredible 96.01m off the ground, three times as high as the stadium itself.
   c) The fastest kick ever taken in a competitive match (meaning the ball travelled at the highest speed once kicked). Immediately after impact, the ball was travelling at 96.01 miles per hour.
   d) The furthest distance a football has ever been kicked before hitting the ground, 96.01m, in a competitive match.

14. In 2020, Christine Sinclair broke the record for most international goals scored, after she netted 185 goals for Canada. Can you help break down the statistics of her incredible record?

On what day of the week did she score the most goals (clue: most international matches are played in midweek)?

a) Saturday
b) Sunday
c) Wednesday
d) Friday

In what month did she score the most goals (clue: tournaments are played every other summer but qualifying matches and friendlies are played every spring and autumn)?

a) March
b) June
c) July
d) October

In what period of the match did she score the most goals?

a) Minutes 1–15
b) Minutes 31–45+
c) Minutes 60–75
d) Minutes 76–90+

15. **One of the most common concepts used by football statisticians is "expected goals", often abbreviated to "xG", which is a number between 0 and 1. If a player at a certain moment of a game has 0.25xG, this means that the player ...**

a) ... has a 25 per cent chance they will score a goal during the match.

b) ... has a 25 per cent chance to win the game.

c) ... has a 25 per cent chance of scoring a goal whenever that player is at that position.

d) ... has a 25 per cent chance of scoring a goal at that moment.

16. **Which player, after helping Bayern Munich win the 2021 German Bundesliga title, completed a run of nine seasons in a row winning league titles? He also played for Paris Saint-Germain (France) and Juventus (Italy).**

a) Zlatan Ibrahimović

b) Edison Cavani

c) Kingsley Coman

d) Juan Bernat

17. **Dutch striker Vivianne Miedema has scored more goals for the Netherlands national team than any other player. She also raced to 100 goals in her first 110 games for Arsenal – what made that achievement even more impressive?**

a) She didn't score a single penalty.

b) She scored a record 10 hat-tricks in one season.

c) She spent her first season playing in defence.

d) Seventy-two of her goals were scored in matches away from home.

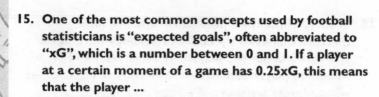

18. **Teams can measure player performance during matches thanks to a piece of technology worn like a sports bra under the players' team shirts. The device measures player data in real time and can tell coaches when players are short of energy and might have increased injury risk. The technology used is known as LPS – what does LPS stand for?**

   a) Let Players Sweat
   b) Local Positioning System
   c) Lightweight Programming Solution
   d) Live Player Statistics

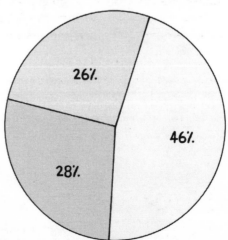

19. **What World Cup statistic links Italy, Brazil, France and Mexico?**

   a) One player has played for all four teams.
   b) They have scored the most goals in the competition.
   c) They have hosted the tournament more than once.
   d) They have won the tournament more than once.

20. **Football matches can end with a win for the home side, a win for the away side, or a draw. The pie-chart below shows how Premier League matches are split between these three results. Which section refers to which result?**

   a) Home win
   b) Away win
   c) Draw

26%

46%

28%

CLEVER COACHES

Motivator. Tactician. Teacher. Public speaker. Transfer expert. Media darling. Fan favourite. Psychologist. Parental figure. Talent improver. Expectation manager. Substitute strategist. The role of the football coach is a complicated one: if the team wins, the players get the credit; if they lose, it's the coach's fault. One of the most successful coaches of all time, the Italian Giovanni Trapattoni, once said that a good coach can make a team 10 per cent better, but a bad coach can make it 30 per cent worse. Trap was a maths genius as well as a top coach. Bravo, Gio!

We remember the best coaches in history because they are the ones that made that 10 per cent difference – elevating the team's performance to deliver results and trophies. They are the ones who outwitted their opponents with smart tactics and used motivational and managerial techniques to improve their players. Some coaches were great players themselves, some were former teachers, but often, football's best coaches today are those who have dedicated their whole career to the craft.

Now it's your turn to put on your coaching hat: can you defeat these puzzling questions? What tactics will you use? Get yourself motivated and go for it! You've got this!

1. **The coaches below have all won the World Cup this century. Can you match them to the countries they were in charge of:**

COACH		COUNTRY
a) Vicente del Bosque	1)	Brazil 2002
b) Didier Deschamps	2)	Italy 2006
c) Jill Ellis	3)	Germany 2007
d) Joachim Loew	4)	Spain 2010
e) Marcello Lippi	5)	Japan 2011
f) Silvia Neid	6)	Germany 2014
g) Norio Sasaki	7)	France 2018
h) Luiz Felipe Scolari	8)	USA 2019

2. **In the early-1900s, English coaches travelled to Europe to educate teams with innovative methods to improve players. Among them was William Garbutt, who won Italy's first-ever league title with Genoa in 1924. What was Garbutt called by his players – a term still used by Italian players when referring to their manager?**

   a) Gentleman
   b) Boss
   c) Sir
   d) Mister

3. **The Premier League between its inception in 1992 and 2022 was never won by a team coached by an Englishman. The league title has been won most times by a coach (or coaches) from which country?**

   a) Italy
   b) Portugal
   c) Scotland
   d) Spain

4. **The Argentinian Marcelo Bielsa, who has coached his country, Chile and several sides in Europe, is considered one of the most influential coaches in the world. At Leeds United his success and his many eccentricities made him adored by fans. Unlike other coaches he did not sit in the dugout when watching his team play. What did he sit on instead?**

   a) A cardboard box
   b) A football
   c) A space hopper
   d) An upturned bucket

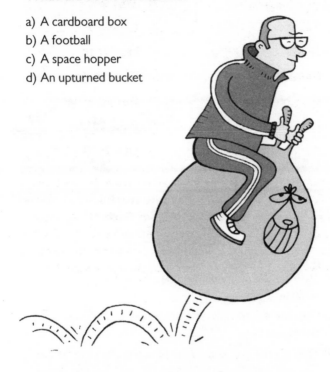

5. **Some of the greatest modern-day coaches in the world, including Pep Guardiola, Carlo Ancelotti, Diego Simeone and Antonio Conte, all played in the same position when they were younger. What was it?**

   a) Goalkeeper
   b) Defender
   c) Midfielder
   d) Forward

6. What is the German word given to the tactical system popularized by German coach Jürgen Klopp in which a team's players immediately try to get the ball back as soon as they have lost it, rather than falling back and regrouping?

a) Schadenfreude
b) Gegenpressing
c) Tiki-taka
d) Kugelschreiber

7. What links Vittorio Pozzo (Italy coach 1929–1948) and Jill Ellis (USA women's coach 2014–2019)?

a) They are the only people to have won the World Cup as a player and a coach.
b) They are the only international coaches to appoint their children as captain.
c) They are the only player-managers to compete in the World Cup.
d) They are the only coaches to have won two World Cups.

8. Can you place the following managers in the order of who coached the most matches in the Premier League?

a) Rafa Benítez
b) Sir Alex Ferguson
c) Jürgen Klopp
d) José Mourinho
e) Arsène Wenger

9. **Former Manchester United coach Sir Alex Ferguson used the phrase "squeaky bum time" to mean the nerve-wracking moments towards the end of a match or competition when more than one team can win. But what is "Fergie time"?**

   a) 3pm on a Saturday afternoon
   b) An afternoon of celebration spent at the horse races
   c) Excessive added time given by the referee in order for a team to score a late goal
   d) Time during which play is stopped by coaches arguing on the touchline

10. **The job of the coach is to choose the tactics, pick the players and explain those decisions to the public before and after each game. Those decisions are often explained with an interview conducted in front of lots of journalists who report what the coach says. What is this interview called?**

    a) Fireside chat
    b) Sports seminar
    c) Media postmortem
    d) Press conference

11. **Coaches are always asked for their opinions, and often they say memorable things. Can you finish these famous phrases?**

    Pep Guardiola: "We do not pass to move the ball, we pass to move the ..."

    a) ... crowd.
    b) ... opposition.
    c) ... players.
    d) ... goalkeeper.

    Emma Hayes: "When a goose gets injured, two birds always accompany it down to the ground. Just as geese do, we must ..."

    a) ... migrate to the other side.
    b) ... lay our golden eggs.
    c) ... flap our wings in unison.
    d) ... support each other.

12. **Dutch coach Sarina Wiegman was the first player to win 100 caps for her country, the first coach to win FIFA's Best award twice, and the first non-British permanent head coach of the England Lionesses team. What job did she take early in her career which she said improved her communication, organization and emotional intelligence?**

    a) Police officer
    b) Politician
    c) Landscape gardener
    d) PE teacher

13. **English coach Nigel Pearson, who helped build the Leicester team that won the 2016 Premier League title, has a reputation as a tough character. What remarkable thing did he once do on holiday?**

    a) He fought off a pack of wild dogs that attacked him while hiking alone in the mountains of Transylvania.
    b) He completed an ultramarathon in the Australian outback by riding on the back of an emu for 6 miles.
    c) He dived into rapids and saved a man from drowning in Saskatchewan.
    d) He mistakenly shot himself in both legs on a clay-pigeon shooting trip in Scotland.

14. **What title-winning feat links José Mourinho, Pep Guardiola, Carlo Ancelotti and Eric Gerets? They have all won league titles:**

    a) Managing teams they used to play for
    b) In four different countries
    c) Without signing any new players
    d) Without losing a single match

15. **Which of the following motivational techniques has coach Brendan Rodgers used in order to inspire his team?**

    a) Promised a player a hat if he scored a hat-trick
    b) Drew a picture of a stick man wearing a crown, in order to show a footballer that he is a master of his own destiny
    c) Brought a box of ants to the training ground, in order to explain the benefits of working together
    d) Written "You're the best" on pieces of paper, folded them up and put them inside players' boots.

16. **Beverly Priestman was assistant coach of England women's team before being appointed head coach of Canada women's team in 2020. What happened next?**

a) She picked herself in goal in a 0–0 draw with Mexico.
b) Canada beat USA for the first time in 20 years in the 2020 Olympics and went on to win the gold medal.
c) She grew her players' resilience by telling them to practise with their laces tied together.
d) She shaved a maple leaf into the back of her hair and dyed it red to match the Canadian flag.

17. **Chelsea beat Villarreal in the 2021 European Super Cup after a penalty shoot-out. What unusual thing did Chelsea coach Thomas Tuchel do in the final minute of extra time?**

a) He pretended to have a heart attack and writhed on the touchline, thus ruining the concentration of the opposition.
b) He ordered everyone on the bench to start dancing the hokey cokey.
c) He substituted off goalkeeper Édouard Mendy and brought on second-choice goalkeeper Kepa Arrizabalaga, the first time in a European final that a goalkeeper has been brought on just for the shoot-out.
d) He took out a small cross, stuck it by the touchline, kneeled and prayed.

THE HOKEY COKEY

18. **English coach Graham Potter used to challenge his players to do different tasks to get used to being uncomfortable with new situations, in the belief it would help them build resilience on the pitch. He even joined in with their activities, which included:**

    a) Performing the ballet *Swan Lake* in front of a live audience
    b) Learning how to lasso a reindeer
    c) Singing at a pop concert for fans
    d) All of the above

19. **Some teams use specialist coaches to help them succeed in certain parts of the game. Which of the following roles exist?**

    a) Throw-in coach
    b) Substitutions coach
    c) Restarts coach
    d) All of the above

20. **Which of the following people was appointed head coach at a top-division team aged 28, by far the youngest to coach at that level in one of Europe's big five leagues?**

    a) Julian Nagelsmann at Hoffenheim (Germany)
    b) Carlo Ancelotti at Bologna (Italy)
    c) Corinne Diacre at Clermont (France)
    d) Gareth Southgate at Middlesbrough (England)

CLUB CULTURE

Everyone is different. Alex likes to wake up early and work before breakfast. Ben sometimes picks his toenails in the bath. These differences make us special and interesting. Football clubs are also different. In this chapter we'll celebrate the things that make all clubs unique in their own particular way.

A football club is more than just its results. Players and coaches come and go, fortunes go up and down. What remains are its traditions. And of course its fans! We are attached to our clubs because of what they stand for, and

the sense of belonging they give, as much as the trophies they win. Our love for a team may reach its peak when a goal goes in but this devotion lasts forever.

Clubs have their own "culture", by which we mean they do things their own way. Every club is unique, with its own kit, mascot, motto, nicknames, in-jokes and songs. Some clubs have great local support, others have a global appeal. Different clubs have different beginnings and different histories. As a fan, you are part of what makes it special now – and you will be a part of its future too!

1. **Gunnersaurus at Arsenal and Mighty Red at Liverpool are two of the best-known mascots in Britain. Try your hand at matching these ten mascots to their clubs:**

MASCOT	CLUB
a) Billy Badger	1) Aston Villa
b) Captain Blade	2) Sheffield United
c) Chirpy Cockerel	3) Blackburn Rovers
d) Crusty the Pie	4) Fulham
e) Filbert Fox	5) Wigan
f) Hammerhead	6) Leicester City
g) Hercules and Bella the Lions	7) Plymouth Argyle
h) Pilgrim Pete	8) Stoke City
i) Pottermus Hippo	9) Tottenham Hotspur
j) Rover the Dog	10) West Ham

2. **The oldest national leagues in the world are the English and Scottish leagues, which were founded in 1888 and 1890. Which three of the following teams were in the 1889–9 English first division?**

   a) Aston Villa
   b) Chelsea
   c) Everton
   d) Manchester United
   e) Wolverhampton Wanderers

Which three of the following teams were in the 1890–91 Scottish first division?

a) Aberdeen
b) Celtic
c) Heart of Midlothian
d) Hibernian
e) Rangers

3. **What vegetable did Chelsea fans use to throw on the pitch before the club banned the practice in 2007?**

    a) Peas
    b) Broccoli
    c) Celery
    d) Potatoes

4. **For each of the countries below, two clubs are listed. One is based on the mainland of that country, and one is based on an island. Can you work out which is which? For an extra point, name the island!**

COUNTRY	CLUB
a) France	1) Copenhagen
b) Spain	2) Ajaccio
c) Portugal	3) Real Mallorca
d) Italy	4) Nacional
e) Denmark	5) Sampdoria
	6) Midtjylland
	7) Monaco
	8) Benfica
	9) Real Valladolid
	10) Palermo

5. **Which Premier League team does Prince William support? He said he chose this team because he wanted to be different from his school friends, who mostly supported Chelsea and Manchester United, and he wanted to support "a mid-table team that could give me more roller-coaster moments".**

    a) Aston Villa
    b) Everton
    c) Leeds
    d) Brighton & Hove Albion

6. **What is special about Southern United FC, from Otago, New Zealand?**

    a) The club plays football with a rugby ball.
    b) Its home is the Kiwi Stadium, which is in the shape of a giant kiwi fruit.
    c) The club only picks hobbits.
    d) It is the most southerly club to play in a country's top tier.

7. **What does the Yellow Wall at Borussia Dortmund's stadium refer to?**

    a) A spot in the dressing-room which the home team touch for good luck before going onto the pitch
    b) A special seating area for players who have been sent off to cool down
    c) One of the largest and loudest stands in Europe, positioned behind one goal where around 25,000 Dortmund fans, wearing the team's yellow shirts, watch games
    d) An area in the training-ground area where players improve their skills: the ball comes to them at speed from different angles in the wall, and they have to control it and return it

8. **Milan's two big teams, Internazionale and AC Milan, traditionally drew their support from two opposite sides of the Milanese population. Which two sides?**

   a) Rich and poor
   b) North and south
   c) Tall and short
   d) Happy and sad

9. **What is Arsenal fan Robbie Lyle's claim to fame?**

   a) He was made official Poet Laureate of the club after inventing the chant "We love you Arsenal" at age eight.
   b) He started Arsenal Fan TV, a YouTube channel for Arsenal fans to talk about the club, which has become the most successful football fan site in the world, with more than a million subscribers and more than a billion views.
   c) He invented the red and white "Gunner bun" (a cake made with strawberry and vanilla icing) which is now sold in their thousands outside the stadium on match days.
   d) He knitted the world's largest football scarf, which is 1km long, and which once a season is wrapped around the Emirates Stadium.

10. **Which famous pop singer supports Tottenham Hotspur and even unfurled a Spurs banner during a live concert?**

    a) Harry Styles
    b) Adele
    c) Ed Sheeran
    d) Beyoncé

11. Match the famous chants to the correct clubs.

CHANT

CLUB

a) "I'm forever blowing bubbles."

1) West Ham

b) "You'll never walk alone."

2) Millwall

c) "No one likes us, we don't care."

3) Hibernian

d) "Sunshine on Leith."

4) Liverpool

e) "Glad all over."

5) Crystal Palace

12. What is interesting about the history of the Milton Keynes Dons?

a) For more than 100 years, the club had another name and were based in a different city before moving to Milton Keynes in 2003.

b) The club is the first English club founded in the 21st century to play in a professional league.

c) The club was formed by the merging of three clubs, Milton, Keynes and Doncaster.

d) The club founder was called Milton Keynes and he insisted the club was named after him and his son, Don.

13. How do Real Sociedad fans who are not in the stadium know when their team has scored?

a) The club sets off fireworks outside the stadium.

b) The club plays the Basque national anthem through speakers all over the city of San Sebastián.

c) The club fire off rockets after every goal; one for the away team, two for the home team.

d) Every TV and radio station in the region broadcasts every home match.

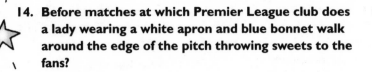

14. **Before matches at which Premier League club does a lady wearing a white apron and blue bonnet walk around the edge of the pitch throwing sweets to the fans?**

    a) West Ham
    b) Crystal Palace
    c) Everton
    d) Southampton

15. **Match these players to the clubs they are all-time top-scorers for.**

PLAYER	CLUB
a) Cristiano Ronaldo	1) Liverpool
b) Eusébio	2) Barcelona Femeni
c) Lionel Messi	3) Chelsea
d) Sergio Agüero	4) Benfica
e) Jenni Hermoso	5) Manchester City
f) Ian Rush	6) Real Madrid
g) Frank Lampard	7) Barcelona

16. **What links the clubs JVW, which plays in the top tier of South African women's football, and Akademija Pandev, which plays in the top tier of the North Macedonian men's league?**

a) Five of the players in JVW are married to players from Academija Pandev, after the Macedonians went to South Africa for pre-season training in 2020 and ended up staying a year because of Covid.

b) They are the only teams in the world that insist all players are vegan.

c) They were both founded by their country's greatest-ever players, Janine van Wyk and Goran Pandev, who named the teams after themselves.

d) They are both owned by Dua Lipa, who has South African and North Macedonian roots.

17. **Since West Bromwich Albion agreed a new shirt sponsor in 2018, their mascot has dressed as what household item to support the partnership?**

a) A kettle
b) A boiler
c) A television
d) A chair

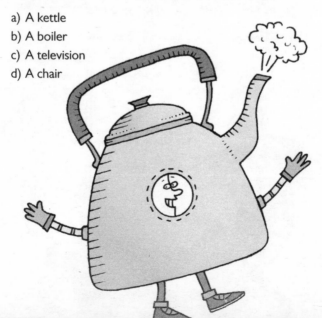

18. **Which team has the oldest club song in the world? The song, called "On the Ball, City", is older than the club itself, as it was sung for other sports teams from the area from the 1890s.**

    a) Leicester City
    b) Bristol City
    c) Manchester City
    d) Norwich City

19. **Scottish team Rangers were named after which English team in 1872?**

    a) Cycling club Northampton Rangers
    b) Rowing club Hull Rangers
    c) Rugby club Swindon Rangers
    d) Squash club Chester Rangers

20. **Which English team's fans sing a song about bread, which goes like this: "Bread! Bread! Who will buy my bread? Long ones, short ones, some as big as my head!"**

    a) Stoke City
    b) Derby County
    c) Shrewsbury Town
    d) Bolton Wanderers

ootball history is made by great games. These fabulous fixtures are the ones in which heroes are made and reputations are won or lost. Football fans never forget the biggest of big games. We all remember sitting on the edge of our seats when watching the final of, say, the World Cup or the Champions League. But it is not just knockout competitions that throw up colossal clashes. Leagues have big games too, such as a bout between the title contenders, or maybe the last match of a season if the title depends on those final results. A great match is often like a Hollywood

thriller – both are spectacles that last for about the same time. They contain intrigue, adventure, goodies and baddies (depending on who you are supporting) and usually a dramatic finale!

Tournament finals and top-of-the-table clashes are always big games, but there are many other ways for matches to be momentous. All games are exciting because they are unpredictable, and sometimes the most remarkable things do happen. We'll be testing you about some brilliant bouts. Are you a match for this contest? Let's play-off!

1. **Matches between traditional rivals are always momentous. Some of these clashes even have their own names. Pair the following matches with the teams that play in them.**

   MATCH

   a) El Clásico

   b) Le Classique

   c) Der Klassiker

   d) Il Derby della Madonnina

   e) El Superclásico

   f) De Topper

   TEAMS

   1) Ajax v. PSV

   2) Boca Juniors v. River Plate

   3) Bayern Munich v. Borussia Dortmund

   4) Marseilles v. Paris Saint-Germain

   5) AC Milan v. Inter Milan

   6) Real Madrid v. Barcelona

2. **The Euro 2020 final between England and Italy was one of England's most important matches of recent years, the first time they reached the final of a major tournament in more than half a century. The nail-biting game ended 1–1 and Italy won 3–2 on penalties. What did coach Gareth Southgate say after the game?**

   a) "I can't believe the lads didn't score! After everything I told them to do! What complete losers!"
   b) "I'm as sick as a parrot. In fact, I'm as sick as a parrot that has caught coronavirus, is infested with fleas and has been run over by a double-decker bus."
   c) "It's down to me. I decided on the penalty-takers based on what we've done in training, and nobody is on their own."
   d) "I am so upset I want to see my mummy. Waaaaaaa!"

3. **The Champions League final is the biggest match of the European football season. What links the 2019 final (won by Liverpool) and the 2021 final (won by Chelsea)?**

   a) Both finals went to penalties.
   b) Both finals were between two English teams.
   c) Both finals featured seven goals.
   d) Both finals were against Bayern Munich.

4. **The USA have won the last two Women's World Cups in a row, sealing victory with an incredible game (5–2) in 2015 and winning 2–0 in 2019. Which teams did they beat in the finals?**

   a) Canada and Brazil
   b) Germany and France
   c) Sweden and England
   d) Japan and the Netherlands

5. **What is the name given to a crucial league game between two teams who are in similar positions in the table?**

   a) Two-pointer
   b) Three-pointer
   c) Four-pointer
   d) Six-pointer

6. **In 1986, Argentina beat England 2–1 in one of the most dramatic World Cup games of all time. The game is famous for the two goals scored by Diego Maradona: the "Hand of God", in which he punched the ball into the net without the referee seeing, and the "goal of the century" in which he dribbled through the entire English defence and dummied the keeper. What had happened a few years before between England and Argentina that stoked an intense rivalry between the countries, and contributed to the heightened atmosphere of the game?**

a) England beat Argentina 1–0 in the 1982 World Cup final, with captain Nobby Stiles scoring a controversial last-minute winner with his dentures, a goal nicknamed the "Gnashers of God".

b) Argentina invaded the Falkland Islands, a group of islands in the south Atlantic that belonged to the UK in 1982, resulting in a short war between the two nations.

c) The musical *Evita*, about the former Argentinian First Lady Eva Perón, caused huge offence to Argentines when it was premiered in London in 1976.

d) A boat race at the 1980 Olympics ended up with British and Argentinian crews involved in a mass brawl, which is the origin of the phrase "argy-bargy".

7. **Can you match the scorelines to these World Cup finals?**

WC FINAL

a) 1930, Uruguay v. Argentina (in Uruguay, the first-ever World Cup final)

b) 1958, Brazil v. Sweden (in Sweden, Brazil's first World Cup win)

c) 1966, England v. West Germany (in London, England's only World Cup triumph)

d) 1970, Brazil v. Italy (in Mexico City, Brazil's third World Cup win with the team often described as the best of all time)

e) 1986, Argentina v. West Germany (in Mexico, Argentina's second World Cup win, this time with Diego Maradona)

f) 1998, France v. Brazil (in Paris, France's first World Cup win)

g) 2010, Spain v. Netherlands (in South Africa, Spain's first World Cup win)

h) 2018, France v. Croatia (in Russia, France win for the second time)

SCORELINE

1) 1-0

2) 3-0

3) 3-2

4) 4-1

5) 4-2

6) 4-2

7) 5-2

8) 4-2

8. **The 2020 Women's Champions League final made history as the winning team sealed a sequence of an incredible five Champions League trophies in a row. Which team won it?**

a) Chelsea

b) Manchester City

c) Real Madrid

d) Olympique Lyonnais Féminin

9. **The Miracle of Istanbul is the name given to the 2005 Champions League final in which a British team beat AC Milan after an extraordinary comeback. The team was trailing 3–0 at half-time but managed to score three goals in a magical six-minute period in the second half, and then won on penalties. Which team was it?**

   a) Liverpool
   b) Manchester United
   c) Chelsea
   d) Celtic

10. **The 1966 Men's World Cup final between England and West Germany, and the 2015 Women's World Cup final between the USA and Japan, were classic matches which both featured what amazing achievement?**

    a) Players in both matches scored a hat-trick (Geoff Hurst for England and Carli Lloyd for the USA).
    b) Both winning teams came from 2–0 behind to win (England 4–2, USA 5–2).
    c) A player making their first appearance for the team scored the winning goal (Alan Ball for England and Tobin Heath for the USA).
    d) Both captains played for West Ham (Bobby Moore for England and Carli Lloyd for the USA).

11. **In 2020, Bayern Munich beat Barcelona 8–2 in a dramatic Champions League knockout match. In the last five minutes, the game was particularly upsetting for Barcelona fans – why?**

    a) Gerard Piqué and Lionel Messi were sent off.
    b) Bayern scored two goals, both by Philippe Coutinho, who was on loan from Barcelona at the time.
    c) Bayern Munich scored five goals.
    d) The fans were told they had to stay the night in the stadium because of a nearby fire.

12. **Spanish club Villarreal beat Manchester United in the 2021 Europa League final which culminated in a record-breaking penalty shoot-out. What happened?**

   a) The first nine players all missed their penalties.

   b) The referee sent off the United goalkeeper for jumping off his line and Villarreal took three penalties without any goalkeeper to stop them.

   c) The first 21 players all scored their penalties and the United goalkeeper missed his.

   d) United coach Ole Gunnar Solskjaer, a former striker for Norway, subbed himself on to take a penalty – and scored.

13. **On their way to winning the 2019 Women's World Cup, USA beat Thailand by a record-breaking score (for a World Cup) in the group stage. What was the score?**

   a) 10–2

   b) 12–3

   c) 13–0

   d) 9–1

14. **In 2014, the Faroe Islands beat Greece 1–0 in a European Championships qualifier. Why has that result gone down in giant-killing history?**

   a) It was the first time the Faroes had ever won a match.

   b) It was the biggest shock in terms of population size difference between two countries: 48,000 people live in the Faroe Islands compared with Greece's population of 11 million.

   c) It was the biggest shock in terms of FIFA world rankings margin between two countries: Greece was ranked 18th and the Faroes 187th in the world.

   d) It was the biggest shock in terms of area size between countries: the Faroes is about 1 per cent the size of Greece.

15. One of the biggest World Cup shocks ever was Brazil's 7–1 defeat in the 2014 World Cup semi-final, held in Brazil. It was the only time in Brazil's history a side had scored seven goals against them and also ended a run of 62 unbeaten matches played at home. Which team beat them in that semi-final?

a) Argentina
b) Germany
c) England
d) Uruguay

16. Which Premier League team was beaten 9–0 by Leicester in October 2019, and, with the same coach in charge, lost by the same scoreline to Manchester United in February 2021?

a) Newcastle
b) Everton
c) Brighton
d) Southampton

17. Romanian club Steaua Bucharest beat Barcelona in the 1984 European Cup final. In that match Steaua goalkeeper Helmuth Duckadam did something that had never been done before and has not been done since in a knockout competition. What was it?

a) In the shoot-out, he saved four penalties in a row.
b) He became the first keeper to score a hat-trick.
c) In the shoot-out, he positioned himself with his back to the penalty-taker and flashed his bottom when the player started his run-up.
d) He scored a goal from a goal kick.

18. **In 2017, England won the Under-17 World Cup after coming from 0–2 down to beat Spain 5–2 in the final. It was the first time England had ever gone past the quarter-finals, let alone go on to win the final in such dramatic circumstances. Which future Premier League star scored two goals in the final and was named Man of the Match?**

    a) Callum Hudson-Odoi
    b) Jadon Sancho
    c) Marc Guéhi
    d) Phil Foden

19. **What was momentous about the match between Claypole and Victoriano Arenas in the Argentinian fifth tier in 2011?**

    a) The referee showed the red card 36 times, sending off all the players, substitutes and coaches.
    b) The match went to a penalty shoot-out and, after 48 kicks each, Claypole won 19–18.
    c) The match ended 100–0 after the Victoriano Arenas players sat down in protest at the referee.
    d) The ball never touched the pitch during the first half because the players decided to head the ball to each other rather than kick it.

20. **Can you match these local derbies to the cities and countries in which they take place?**

LOCAL DERBY	LOCATION
a) Al Ahly v. Zamalek	1) Rio de Janeiro, Brazil
b) Celtic v. Rangers	2) Cairo, Egypt
c) Mohun Bagan v. East Bengal	3) Kolkata, India
d) Flamengo v. Fluminense	4) Rome, Italy
e) Lazio v. Roma	5) Glasgow, Scotland

RULES AND REFEREES

All sports need rules, and people to enforce these rules. Otherwise there would be chaos. In football, the rules are called the Laws of the Game, and the enforcers are the referees. A ref's job is to be fair and strict, and not to get in the way of the ball!

In 1863, the Football Association was founded in order to establish standard rules for the sport. Originally, there were thirteen laws, written over four pages. Since then they have been modified many times in order to make the game fairer and more exciting. There are now seventeen laws with so many rules and directions that the current Laws of the Game runs to well over 100 pages.

Being a referee is a demanding job. You need to have amazing powers of concentration, observation, assertiveness and resolve. At every match you will be shouted at, pleaded with and wound up by fans. Yet great football matches need great referees. Football relies on the rules being applied equally to both sides.

Below we're going to test you on some of the laws. Now you get a chance to be ref. *Peep peep*!

1. **In the first Laws of the Game, from 1863, there was no rule on the length or width of a football pitch. The laws did state, however, that the pitch should contain which one of the following four elements?**

   a) The penalty spots
   b) Goals with crossbars
   c) Corner flags
   d) The centre-circle

2. **How were fouls awarded before 1891?**

   a) Players admitted fouls as a matter of honour, and gave the ball to the opposing team.
   b) Each team had its own umpire who would consult a referee on the sideline if there was a foul.
   c) The team coach would make the decision and promised to always act honestly.
   d) There were no fouls awarded.

3. **Let's play "Goal or No Goal?" Can you score a goal from the following scenarios? For each option, answer "Goal" or "No Goal".**

   a) First touch from kick-off
   b) The ball bursts before it crosses the line.
   c) A goal kick
   d) A throw-in
   e) A dog runs onto the pitch and touches the ball.
   f) A penalty is awarded during normal time. The penalty-taker, instead of shooting at the goal, passes the ball to a team-mate.
   g) The scorer has their shirt untucked.

4. The offside rule is often called the most complicated rule in football. Complete the sentence so as to give the best explanation for it. A player is offside if they receive the ball ...

a) ... in the opposition half from a pass in their own half.

b) ... while ahead of the second-last opponent when the pass is made.

c) ... in the opposition area from a goal kick or throw-in.

d) ... when they are level with the ball and the last opponent.

5. Referees use hand signals so it is clear to players and spectators exactly what decision has been made. Match the signal to the meaning:

a) Goal
b) Penalty
c) Play on
d) Direct free kick
e) VAR check

6. You might think you know most of the rules in football, but some are tricky! Which one of the following football rules is correct?

a) You can get booked for illegally celebrating a goal even if the goal is disallowed.

b) If a team has a player sent off, they have to take one fewer penalty in a shoot-out.

c) A match can start if one team only has six players.

d) Goalkeepers are allowed to hold on to the ball for a maximum of 10 seconds.

7. What is the only scenario in which an assistant referee can go onto the pitch?

a) To break up a fight which endangers the referee

b) To help the referee mark out 10 yards at a free kick

c) To carry off an injured player who is being substituted

d) To tell the goalkeeper to stay on his line before a penalty kick

8. **During normal time, a striker hits a penalty against the post, reacts quickly and hits the ball in the net directly from the rebound. What decision does the referee give?**

   a) Goal
   b) Indirect free kick to the defending team
   c) Direct free kick to the attacking team
   d) Retake the penalty

9. **Which of the following objects must a referee always have in his pocket?**

   a) Energy bar
   b) Handkerchief
   c) Coin
   d) Battery

10. **Bibiana Steinhaus, who retired in 2020, was the first female ref to referee in the Bundesliga. She also refereed the 2011 Women's World Cup final. But what was her job before she became a referee?**

    a) Police chief inspector
    b) Teacher
    c) Traffic warden
    d) Footballer

11. **Referee shirts come in different colours. But their shorts are always:**

    a) Black
    b) White
    c) Grey
    d) Pink

12. **When he was coach of Chelsea, José Mourinho criticized a referee, which resulted in a stadium ban for two Champions League matches. How did he get around the ban?**

a) He dressed up as the referee and was allowed in.
b) He hid in the bottom of a laundry basket so he could get to the dressing room.
c) He pretended to be one of the players.
d) He spent the whole night before the game sleeping in the dressing room.

13. **VAR, or Video Assistant Referee, was introduced to help reduce referee mistakes. To help with VAR, there is now an RRA. But what does RRA stand for?**

a) Retired Referees' Academy
b) Recommended Referee Assistant
c) Radio Referees Association
d) Referee Review Area

14. **There was a slight change in the rules at the first Women's World Cup, held in 1991. What was it?**

    a) Each team was allowed to make six substitutions.
    b) Matches lasted 80 minutes instead of the normal 90 minutes.
    c) There was no extra time; drawn games went straight to a penalty shoot-out.
    d) Each team was allowed to pick two goalkeepers to handle the ball in the area.

15. **Blind football is a Paralympic sport. All of the following are rules in the sport except one. Which one?**

    a) Every player except for the goalkeeper has to wear a blindfold.
    b) The coaches must stand with their backs to the game.
    c) The players must shout before they tackle an opponent.
    d) The ball has a bell in it so players know where it is.

16. **As of 2022, which of the following men's competitions is the only one never to have had a female referee?**

   a) Bundesliga
   b) Ligue I
   c) Premier League
   d) Champions League
   e) World Cup Qualifiers
   f) FIFA Club World Cup

17. **A direct free kick is a kick from which a goal can be scored without any other player touching the ball. An indirect free kick has to touch another player before going in. Which of the following fouls would result in a direct or indirect free kick?**

   a) Handball
   b) Dangerous play
   c) Tripping an opponent
   d) Holding back an opponent's shirt
   e) Swearing
   f) Goalkeeper picking up a back-pass

18. **How did Welsh referee Clive Thomas infuriate Brazil fans at the 1978 World Cup?**

   a) He sent off their coach Cláudio Coutinho, banning him from giving a half-time team-talk.
   b) He blew his whistle half a second before Zico scored what would have been a winning goal.
   c) He disallowed three goals for offside because he misunderstood the rule.
   d) He ordered them to change their bright-yellow shirts to black as they hurt his eyes.

19. **Complete the true statement about referees.**

   Based on years of studying referee habits, researchers have concluded that referees tend to …

   a) … favour the home side by awarding them more penalties.
   b) … favour the home side by showing their players fewer yellow cards.
   c) … favour the away side as they feel sorry for them.
   d) … favour neither side.

20. **Some of the following are the real names of referee whistles. Can you blow the whistle on the fakes?**

   a) Wheezer 57
   b) Fox Eclipse
   c) WarbleWizard T2000
   d) Acme 888
   e) Blow-Ninja X
   f) Dolfin F

FABULOUS FASHION

It's time to dress up! This chapter is about football's wardrobe of wonders, by which we mean the clothing used by players, officials and fans. Football shirts come in many colours and are an important part of the identity of clubs and national teams. The Reds! The Blues! The Clarets!

As well as having distinctive colours, football shirts also proudly display the team badge, a symbol that represents the club or national side. Badges can be ancient coats of arms, initials, flags, plants, buildings and even cartoon-like figures. We'll ask the questions – and you'll do the c-rest!

Modern football kits are about science as well as style. Shirts used to be made from cotton but technological advances mean they are now mostly made from man-made materials. Boots also come in many different colours and designs. Don't forget to tie your laces!

One way that footballers can show individuality on the pitch is by having a fancy hairdo. Some players are trendsetters with marvellous manes that change every season. For questions about coiffures, you'll have to use your head!

1. **Most teams play in shirts that are a single colour, or have vertical or horizontal stripes. But some have a distinctive pattern. Match the team to the shirt.**

   a) Blackburn Rovers
   b) Croatia
   c) Peru
   d) Queens Park Rangers
   e) Wycombe Wanderers

   3) Hoops

   1) Halved

   2) Quartered

   5) Sash

   4) Chequered

2. **Sometimes players like to change their hairstyle before a major tournament.**

   What colour did England midfielder Phil Foden dye his hair just before Euro 2020?

   a) Bright blue
   b) Bright yellow
   c) Bright green
   d) Bright red

What colour was Megan Rapinoe's hair when she was top-scorer at the 2019 World Cup?

a) Lilac

b) Maroon

c) Turquoise

d) Emerald

3. **Why do so many coaches wear a suit and tie during big games?**

   a) Because the rules say they have to.

   b) Because their mum told them it looks nice.

   c) So you can tell them apart from the physio.

   d) Because they think it makes them look respectable, serious and important.

4. **What object is often added to a badge to represent an important victory, such as a World Cup or a certain number of domestic league titles?**

   a) Smiley face

   b) Cup

   c) Crown

   d) Star

5. **Half-and-half scarves are often sold outside grounds before big matches. What makes these scarves so special?**

   a) They detach into two.

   b) You turn them upside down at half-time.

   c) They are made from 50 per cent nylon and 50 per cent wool.

   d) They have the names of both teams playing on them.

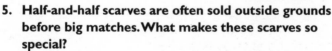

6. Goalkeepers have worn different coloured shirts from their teammates since 1909. Before then, what did goalkeepers wear to make them stand out?

a) Ribbons in their hair
b) A big "G" on the back of their jersey
c) A cap on their head
d) A kilt

7. Sam Widdowson of Nottingham Forest is credited with the invention of shin pads in 1874. He got the idea of protecting his shins from an injury in which other sport?

a) Horse racing
b) Ice hockey
c) Mountain biking
d) Cricket

8. Match the objects on the club badges to the teams they represent.

OBJECT

a) A bear and a strawberry tree
b) A pipe-smoking sailor
c) A green kangaroo
d) A four-leaf clover
e) A Native American chieftain
f) A cannon
g) Two seahorses, a castle and a demi-lion
h) A beacon and two laurel wreaths
i) A tree, three waves and a rose
j) Two hammers crossed over

TEAM

1) Everton
2) Southampton
3) Ghent (Belgium)
4) Bohemians (Czech Republic)
5) Celtic (Scotland)
6) Arsenal
7) West Ham
8) Atlético Madrid (Spain)
9) Sampdoria (Italy)
10) Newcastle

9. **Lions and eagles are probably the two most popular animals used by football teams on their crests. Decide which of the following teams have an eagle or a lion on their crest.**

		LION	EAGLE
a)	Albania	....	....
b)	Aston Villa	....	....
c)	Austria	....	....
d)	Benfica	....	....
e)	Bolivia	....	....
f)	Chelsea	....	....
g)	Crewe Alexandra	....	....
h)	Czech Republic	....	....
i)	England	....	....
j)	Germany	....	....
k)	Nigeria	....	....
l)	Russia	....	....
m)	Mexico	....	....
n)	Middlesbrough	....	....
o)	Netherlands	....	....
p)	Poland	....	....
q)	Scotland	....	....
r)	Serbia	....	....
s)	South Korea	....	....
t)	Spain	....	....
u)	Tunisia	....	....

10. **Boot manufacturers like to give their products exciting and frequently nonsensical names. Which four of the following boot names are real, and which did we make up?**

a) Tekela v3 Energy Streak
b) MegaGoal Fan Party
c) Superfly CR7 Safari
d) Ultra Chasing Adrenaline
e) Ghost Dragon Plague
f) Revolution Boomtime V6
g) Mania Tormentor
h) Scorpion Phantom Racer

11. **At the turn of the nineteenth and twentieth centuries, football began to spread around the world. Many famous European clubs came into existence, and some chose their kit colours based on UK teams. Match the non-English club to the British side that inspired their kits.**

NON-ENGLISH CLUB

a) Athletic Bilbao

b) Juventus

c) Real Madrid

d) Real Betis

e) Sparta Prague

INSPIRATION

1) Arsenal (red and white)

2) Celtic (green and white hoops)

3) Corinthian (white)

4) Notts County (black and white)

5) Southampton (red and white stripes)

12. **Which three countries below wear a national jersey that contains colours from their national flag.**

   a) Honduras
   b) Italy
   c) Algeria
   d) Australia
   e) Peru
   f) Netherlands

13. **The British Ladies Football Team, founded in 1895, was one of the first organized women's teams to play football. They wore baggy bloomers, long-sleeved shirts, and neckties. What did they wear on their heads?**

   a) Helmets
   b) Fruit
   c) Hairnets
   d) Bonnets

14. **Serie A, Italy's top tier, has banned clubs from wearing predominantly green kits from 2022. Why?**

   a) Because the Green party of Italy has trademarked the colour.
   b) Because Serie A's bosses think green tops blend in with the grass, which is confusing for TV viewers, especially colour-blind ones.
   c) So as not to offend the country's many religious believers, since green is a colour associated with both Christianity and Islam.
   d) Because green is a calming colour, and Serie A believes this makes football less exciting to watch.

15. **Spanish third division team La Hoya is based in Murcia, an area famous for growing one food that appears all over its kit. What is the food?**

    a) Bananas
    b) Figs
    c) Broccoli
    d) Carrots

16. **Paris Saint-Germain introduced a home shirt for the 2021–22 season that has a small picture on the front of a US sportsman. What is the sport he is playing?**

    a) American football
    b) Athletics
    c) Baseball
    d) Basketball

17. **In 2020, Australian company Ida Sports launched a revolutionary new football boot. What made it special?**

    a) It was the first football boot specifically designed for women's feet.
    b) It contained a camera on the front to give fans a toe's-eye view of the game.
    c) It was made from kangaroo leather.
    d) It contained a movable spike in the sole that was controlled by the coaching staff, who could use it to send secret messages to the player in Morse code.

18. **Brazilian striker Neymar is known for his outlandish haircuts. Which of the following haircuts has he NOT (yet!) had?**

a) Pink Mohican b) Blond dreadlocks c) Blue top-knot d) Red mullet

19. **Match the tattoo to the player who has it:**

TATOO	PLAYER
a) Himself celebrating a goal, on his back	1) Ederson (Brazil)
b) A huge lion, on his back	2) Neymar (Brazil)
c) A yellow smiley face, behind his ear	3) Leroy Sané (Germany)
d) His sister's face, on his arm	4) Memphis Depay (Netherlands)

20. **Football shirts used to be made from cotton, but are now usually made from polyester, a man-made fabric. What is the main advantage of polyester over cotton for footballers?**

a) It is lighter and absorbs less water.

b) It can be manufactured in a wider variety of different colours.

c) It is smoother on your body.

d) It is more elastic and less likely to rip or stretch out of shape.

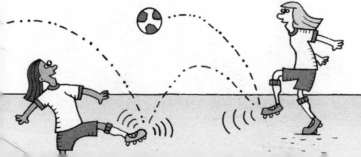

LOVELY LINGO

Advantage! Route one! Park the bus! Nuts! All day long! Football is full of strange and glorious language that only exists on or around the verdant turf, we mean, the pitch. There are certain words or phrases that we only hear, read or say when football is the subject. For example, football's collective phrases include a hatful of chances, a glut of goals or a raft of substitutions. What a madness of phrases!

This challenging chapter contains a flummoxing flurry of quizzical queries about the weird and wonderful lyrical language of this grand game. We will take you

on a journey around the world to explore extraordinary expressions, leaving your tongue twisted and your cranium confronted.

We'll take in funny phrases, ambitious abbreviations, silly similes and even an incredible insult. We'll discover what football is called in other countries and explore the animals, numbers and Latin mottos that are part of the game's unique lexicon.

"*In bocca al lupo*!" as they say in Italy. The phrase translates as "in the mouth of the wolf" – but it also means "good luck".

1. What is the most common nickname for football?

a) The spectacular sport
b) The beautiful game
c) The divine art
d) Footy McFooty-Face

2. When a coach dispenses the "hair dryer treatment", what are they doing?

a) Venting their anger at the team in the dressing room
b) Drying the hair of the players just before they go on the pitch
c) Training in a wind tunnel to build up stamina
d) Mobilizing staff and fans to blow onto the pitch when the other team has a penalty

3. What does it mean when a commentator calls a player "leggy"?

a) The player has long legs.
b) The player can run very fast.
c) The player is very good at defending with their legs.
d) The player looks tired.

4. **In the 1970s, a Scottish side went to Nigeria to play some exhibition games against local sides. They played very badly, and as a result the team's name is now used throughout Nigeria as an insult, meaning "idiot". Which team was it?**

   a) Aberdeen
   b) Celtic
   c) Dundee United
   d) Queen of the South

5. **In most languages, the word for "football" is either "football" or a word that sounds like it, such as "fútbol" in Spanish or "Fußball" in German. In some languages, however, the word is completely different. Match the language below to its translation of "football".**

LANGUAGE		TRANSLATION
a) Croatian	1)	Calcio
b) Finnish	2)	Jalkapallo
c) Greek	3)	Nogomet
d) Italian	4)	Podósfairo

6. **Below is a list of football terms. Some are used by coaches, and some we made up. Can you tell which is which?**

   a) High press
   b) Tackle calculator
   c) Zonal entries contribution
   d) Expected assists
   e) Game state
   f) Save percentage
   g) Dribble danger ratio

7. **Fill in the gap in the following sentence, made by former USA coach Jill Ellis, who was in charge when the team won the 2019 World Cup. She is talking about how she referred to her substitute players during the tournament.**

"When we put up our starting eleven the night before [the game], instead of calling them reserves, we called them ...., and we talked to that group a lot about being ready to step in."

a) Last-minute-Marys
b) Better-late-than-nevers
c) Gamechangers
d) Bench-boomers

8. **In the US, football is called "soccer", a word that emerged in England around the beginning of the twentieth century. What is the origin of the term?**

a) It comes from the word "sock" because the early players used long socks with the team badge.
b) It comes from the word "sock" in the sense of "socking it", or hitting something forcefully, since footballers are allowed to kick the ball as hard as they like.
c) It comes from the word "sucker" because everyone was a sucker for football, meaning they loved it.
d) It comes from the word "association" because football was known as "association football" to distinguish it from "rugby football".

9. What does GOAT stand for?

a) Greatest of All Time
b) Goalscoring Optimists Always Triumph
c) Gobbler of All Trophies
d) Giant on a Thimble

10. Look at the phrases below and the English translations. What is the footballing term that all of these languages are referring to?

LANGUAGE	PHRASE	TRANSLATION
French	Petit pont	Little bridge
Dutch	Poorten	Gate
Arabic	Kobry	Egg
Finnish	Länget	Collar
Spanish	Caño	Spout
Turkish	Beşik	Cradle

a) Header
b) Volley
c) Tackle
d) Nutmeg

11. Match the mottos to the clubs.

MOTTO	CLUB
a) *Més que un club* More than a club	1) Barnsley
b) *Audere est facere* To dare is to do	2) Manchester City
c) *Nil satis nisi optimum* Nothing but the best	3) Arsenal
d) *Superbia in proelia* Pride in battle	4) Tottenham Hotspur
e) *Spectemur agendo* Judge us by our acts	5) Barcelona
f) *Domus clamantium* The home of the shouting men	6) Gillingham
g) *Victoria concordia crescit* Victory grows through harmony	7) Everton

12. A cliché is an overused phrase that is therefore a very predictable and unoriginal thing to say. Can you complete the following football clichés?

a) Over the …

b) Sick as a …

c) At the end of the …

d) A game of two …

1) … halves.

2) … day.

3) … moon.

4) … parrot.

13. British commentators sometimes refer to a shot fired into the top-corner of the goal as hitting the postage stamp, as stamps are found in the top corner of envelopes. What is the equivalent phrase used in Brazil?

a) Where the owl sleeps

b) Pelé's earlobe

c) Attic window

d) In the fruit of a samba dancer's hat

14. Many football phrases are based around numbers. Can you sort the truth from the made-up phrases?

a) 12th man
b) Route four
c) False nine
d) Two-footed tackle
e) 50-50 challenge
f) Nine-pointer
g) Third ball

15. Can you match the following animal-related foreign phrases to their meanings?

PHRASE

a) Spider hands
(used in South Korea)

b) A bee without honey
(used in Turkey)

c) Buffalo push
(used in Belgium)

d) Mouse
(used in Chile)

MEANING

1) A defensive team

2) A header struck with impressive force

3) A player who runs a lot but doesn't contribute much

4) An unbeatable goalkeeper

16. What is a hospital pass?

a) An under-hit pass that leaves a team-mate at risk of being painfully tackled by an opponent

b) A dangerous cross hit behind the defence and in front of the goalkeeper

c) A pass hit so hard that it causes a player to fall over

d) A pass that leads to a goal, giving coaches a big headache

17. A football "pundit" is an expert who appears on TV or radio to express their opinions, or discuss the game in more detail. The word comes from the Hindi word "*pandit*". Which of the following translations gives the correct meaning?

a) A professional moaner

b) A learned religious man

c) An old football player who wishes they were still young

d) Someone skilled in wordplay

18. Match the football terms to their meanings:

TERM	MEANING
a) Howler	1) Area where coaches watch a game
b) Dugout	2) The posts and crossbar
c) Dummy	3) Spectacular banner displayed by fans behind goal
d) Tifo	4) Trick by moving body to fool defender
e) Woodwork	5) Big mistake

19. What is a yo-yo club?

a) A team that trains players by attaching them to a piece of string and pulling against them as they run

b) A team that is regularly promoted and relegated between two divisions, going up and down like a yo-yo

c) A team that has very few supporters, so opposition fans sing "YO-YO" at them, short-hand for "You're on your own"

d) A team that specializes in speedy attacks, running from one end of the pitch to the other like a yo-yo on a string

20. A malapropism is when you mistakenly use the wrong word because it sounds like the right word. For example, if you say "Alex danced the flamingo", when what you actually wanted to say is "Alex danced the flamenco". It can happen with commentators too. Can you find the right word to use in these football examples?

a) Playing matches in Bolivia is a challenge because of the **attitude / altitude**.

b) Whenever the winger gets the ball, the defence looks **petrified / putrified**.

c) The goalkeeper is a player of great **stature / statue** in the squad.

d) The crowd is **anonymous / unanimous** in their dislike of the referee.

KICKS AND TRICKS

There are many ways to skin a cat. There are even more ways to kick a ball! You can chip, hoof, slice, back-heel, volley, toe-poke and many more. The following questions all celebrate the many ways the boots of our favourite players make contact with regulation leather spheres. It's about what happens when foot meets ball!

Different techniques are required for different moments. Corners, goal kicks, free kicks and penalties require special skills, and the best kickers of the ball are highly prized. It takes a lot of practice to learn how to bend a free kick into the goal, so why not start now! And practise your penalties too! As you'll discover, goalkeepers have used many tricks to distract penalty-takers.

Some players have kicks that have become their trademarks. Often these are not just about the feet and legs, but about how the whole body moves. Footballers' tricks can be acrobatic and sometimes very cheeky! Fans love to see players do something audacious and extraordinary – especially when it works.

Now it's your turn to show us how extraordinary you are. Can you dribble past these questions and bicycle-kick them into the net!

1. **Italian midfielder Andrea Pirlo, who played for his country between 2002 and 2015, holds the record for the number of goals scored from a free kick in Serie A. For years, however, he could not get his free kicks quite right until one day, while sitting on the toilet, he realized exactly what he needed to do to perfect his technique. What was it?**

   a) Take a longer run-up
   b) Always look at the corner at which he's aiming
   c) Wipe his bum properly
   d) Strike the ball with only three toes, not the whole foot

2. **What is a name given to a weak shot that moves slowly along the ground?**

   a) Turtle totterer
   b) Snail skidder
   c) Marble wobbler
   d) Pea roller

3. **Which player completed the most successful dribbles in the Premier League in 2020, including fourteen in one game, more than anyone else since dribbling stats were first counted in 2003?**

   a) Adama Traoré
   b) Allan Saint-Maximin
   c) Wilfried Zaha
   d) Jack Grealish

4. **Here we've listed some kicks and tricks named after footballers (with the name of the footballer in brackets), together with the descriptions of what they are. Which one is which?**

TERM

a) Papinade
(French striker
Jean-Pierre Papin)

b) Özil Chop
(German midfielder
Mesut Özil)

c) Zidane Roulette
(French midfielder
Zinedine Zidane)

d) Flo Pass
(Norwegian striker
Jostein Flo)

e) Ronaldo Knuckleball
(Portuguese striker
Cristiano Ronaldo)

MEANING

1) Spinning away from an opponent at speed with one foot on the ball

2) A knock-down from a striker for a midfielder to shoot from the edge of the area

3) A spectacular volley, often struck at an unlikely angle

4) Kicking the ball into the ground so it spins and bounces over an opponent

5) Dipping free kick struck with the laces

5. **You are about to take a free kick and would like the ball to curve to the left. Where should you kick the ball?**

a) On the left side of the ball, giving the ball a clockwise spin
b) On the right side of the ball, giving the ball an anticlockwise spin
c) At the top of the ball, giving the ball top (or forward) spin
d) At the bottom of the ball, giving the ball bottom (or back) spin

6. **What is the name of the trick, associated with Neymar, in which a footballer uses one leg to roll the ball up the back of their other leg and then flicks it forward over their head?**

a) Roly-poly kick
b) Neymar noddle
c) Umbrella kick
d) Rainbow kick

7. **What trick did Russian winger Andrei Kanchelskis get criticized for after performing it for Rangers in the Scottish Cup semi-final in 2000?**

a) He went round the goalkeeper three times before scoring.
b) He stood on the ball and saluted, before crossing for a team-mate to score.
c) He balanced the ball on his head to waste time.
d) He sang his country's national anthem before the game.

8. **Some teams use other tricks to gain an edge over their opponents. In 2018, Norwich City tried something different in their (successful) bid to reach the Premier League. What was it?**

a) Gave visiting players a three-course lunch before matches, so they would be full
b) Played lullabies through the away team's dressing room sound system in order to put them to sleep
c) Painted the away team's dressing-room pink as it is said to have a calming effect
d) Forbade players from scoring in the pre-match warm-up as they wanted to save all goals for the matches

9. **How did Australian midfielder Elise Kellond-Knight score a goal against Norway at the 2019 Women's World Cup?**

a) She back-heeled it into the net from outside the box.

b) She scored direct from a corner kick without it touching any other player.

c) She mistimed her penalty run-up, tripped over and kicked the ball into the goal while lying on the grass.

d) Her shot rebounded off one post, then hit the other post and then went in.

10. **Every year, FIFA presents an award to the player who scored the "most beautiful" goal of the year. Three goals are selected by the public and a panel of experts then votes on the winner. The award is named after a former World Cup top-scorer. Who?**

a) Pelé

b) Sir Bobby Charlton

c) Marta

d) Ferenc Puskás

11. **What remarkable skill did Ireland defender Rory Delap (who played for Stoke City between 2006–13) have that caused fear among his opponents, and that no one has been able to master since?**

a) He could perform a backflip before kicking the ball, which gave the shot extra power.

b) He had joint hypermobility in both his arms and his legs, which enabled him to dribble in directions no one else could.

c) His throw-ins were so powerful, he was able to throw the ball into the penalty area when standing on the touchline anywhere in the opposition half.

d) He could score with either foot from corners.

12. **A player who can score from free kicks and takes excellent corners is known as a ... specialist. What's the missing word?**

a) Set-piece

b) Dead-strike

c) Placed-ball

d) Resting-sphere

13. **One of the most famous football tricks is the Cruyff Turn, named after Dutch winger Johan Cruyff, in which the player drags the ball behind the standing leg to switch direction. Cruyff introduced the move in the 1974 World Cup, in order to get past Sweden defender Jan Olsson. How did Olsson describe the humiliation of being outfoxed by Cruyff in front of a TV audience of millions?**

a) "The worst moment of my career."

b) "The most Swedish moment of my career."

c) "The weirdest moment of my career."

d) "The proudest moment of my career."

14. Free kicks, penalties and corners often lead to goals. But how often?

Out of 100 direct free kicks how many, on average, will result in goals?

a) 2
b) 5
c) 10
d) 15

Out of 100 penalties how many, on average, will result in goals?

a) 48
b) 66
c) 78
d) 90

Out of 100 corners how many, on average, will result in goals?

a) 3
b) 8
c) 12
d) 15

15. When a team is defending a free kick, they often set up a wall, which is a group of players standing next to each other to block a clear path to goal. What is the role of the player known as the "draught excluder" in the wall?

a) Standing on the end of the wall and jumping to stop the ball going in
b) Shouting at the free kick taker to put the player off
c) Lying down behind the wall so if the players in the wall jump the ball cannot go under it
d) Standing at the side that is in the direction of the wind to stop the ball being blown in an unpredictable direction.

16. **Gianni Vio is a former bank manager who became a free kick coach for the Italy national team. He claims to have over 4,000 moves for free kicks and became famous in 2008 when Serie A side Catania scored from one of his routines. The move involved four attacking players forming their own wall behind the defensive wall, to disorientate the goalkeeper. Before the successful free kick was struck, they ran in different directions, and one player did what?**

    a) Fell to the ground and pretended he was injured
    b) Ran back to the ball and scored the free kick
    c) Pulled down his shorts
    d) Shouted "GERONIMO!" at the top of his voice

17. **Goalkeepers use all sorts of tricks to try and distract opponents before facing penalties. Which two tricks have been successfully used by goalkeepers to keep out spot kicks?**

    a) Backflip during player's run-up
    b) Ripping off gloves
    c) Kissing the penalty-taker
    d) Doing a wee in his shorts

18. **What penalty fact links American forward Brandi Chastain with Nigerian forward Obafemi Martins, Romanian midfielder Ianis Hagi and German defender Andreas Brehme?**

a) They have all scored three penalties in one game.

b) They have all missed penalties and scored penalties in the same game.

c) They have all scored chipped "Panenka" penalties in the World Cup.

d) They have all scored penalties with their left foot and right foot.

19. **Argentina forward Martín Palermo has a unique (and infamous) place in penalty history after his exploits in a 1999 Copa América match against Colombia. What happened?**

a) He took three penalties and missed them all.

b) He hit the crossbar so hard it broke.

c) He missed the ball on his run-up, twisted his ankle and had to be substituted.

d) He hit the ball so hard that it knocked out the opposition goalkeeper.

20. **Complete the following sentence about Italy's historic penalty shoot-out victory in the Euro 2020 final.**

Italy were the first team in European Championship history to ...

a) ... beat England in a penalty shoot-out.

b) ... win two penalty shoot-outs in the same tournament.

c) ... score every penalty in a shoot-out.

d) ... win the final after a penalty shoot-out.

WACKY WORLD

Oh no! This is the last chapter of the book. But don't worry, we have saved the best – or at least the strangest – until last! We have already explored what makes football so loved across the world: we have celebrated the game's greatest players, coaches, matches and moments. We've nobbled the names, blasted the balls, recapped the rules and studied the stats. And we think you might have learned a few things along the way. You might even consider yourself a football expert by now. Well, think again!

This is the chapter where anything goes. Welcome to football's wacky world, where fans will do anything to support their team and some players will do anything to, well, keep playing. This chapter worships the weird and wonderful of the game; it celebrates the strange and superstitious, commemorates the curious and recognizes the random and remarkable. You may not know the answers but you will have fun finding them out – and sharing them with your friends and family!

Are you ready to embrace the eccentric? Put on your lucky underpants and let's find out!

1. **What did Birmingham City coach Barry Fry do in the 1990s in order to rid the St Andrew's ground of a curse? The curse had supposedly been set in 1906 by the people who had been forced to move from the land where the stadium was built.**

   a) He fixed crucifixes to the floodlights so the players could handle crosses.
   b) He painted the bottoms of the players' boots blue.
   c) He sprinkled holy water on the coach's seat in the dugout.
   d) He urinated on the corner flag in each of the four corners of the ground.

2. **Which famous British writer was the first-ever goalkeeper of the team that became Portsmouth FC?**

   a) William Shakespeare
   b) Charles Dickens
   c) David Walliams
   d) Sir Arthur Conan Doyle

3. **Marcos Alonso (Spain), Javier Hernández (Mexico) and Patrick Berg (Norway) share an impressive family fact. What is it?**

   a) They all played for their countries when their father was coach.
   b) They all played for their countries, as did both their parents.
   c) They all played for their countries, as did their fathers and grandfathers.
   d) Each of them are one of a set of triplets.

4. **The Isles of Scilly is a group of islands off the coast of Cornwall in south-west England. Which of the curious facts about Scilly's football league is true?**

   a) The five teams go by the hilarious names of the Scilly Sausages, the Scilly Billies, the Scilly Fools, the Scilly Putties and the Scilly Seasons.

   b) It's the smallest league in the world, with only two teams who play each other eighteen times every season.

   c) There are no football pitches in Scilly, so all games are played in Cornwall.

   d) The trophy is a giant Cornish pasty.

5. **What did Marivaldo Francisco da Silva, a supporter of Brazilian team Sport Recife, do to win the 2020 FIFA Fan Award, given to the best fan in the world?**

   a) After moving home to live in a village 40 miles away from the stadium, he continued to attend every Sport home game – walking 11 hours one way, and 11 hours back, because he couldn't afford the bus.

   b) He created the world's largest team banner, which when extended completely covered the entire stadium, including all the stands and the pitch.

   c) He changed his name to Sport 6 Santa Cruz 0 da Silva, after Sport won the Recife local derby against rivals Santa Cruz

   d) He promised that if Sport won the 1994 Brazilian. championship he would clean every window in Recife, a city of 1.5 million people. When the club won, he was true to his word and it took him 25 years to complete the job.

6. **Northern Irishman Jonathan Calderwood is considered the best in the world at what job in football? He was hired by Paris Saint-Germain in 2013 and the following season his work is said to have gained the team an extra sixteen points, helping them win the league title.**

   a) Toe masseur
   b) Nutritionist
   c) Groundsman
   d) Hypnotist

7. **How did Austrian artist Klaus Littmann transform the pitch of Austria Klagenfurt's 30,000-seater stadium in 2019? He hoped the project would make people think about environmental destruction and the future of the Earth.**

   a) He planted 300 fully grown trees on the pitch, so it looked like a forest.
   b) He turned the pitch into a giant ice rink covered by a massive cage and put a polar bear in it.
   c) He put a toilet in the middle of the pitch, and sat on it for 12 hours a day.
   d) He built a huge football out of recycled car parts and decorated it with flowers.

8. **A restaurant in Madeira, the birthplace of Cristiano Ronaldo, has the world's largest collection of what?**

   a) Underpants worn by Cristiano Ronaldo
   b) Posters of Cristiano Ronaldo
   c) Football shirts
   d) Football scarves

9. **Iranian football freestyler Arash Ahmadi Tifakani has two world records: he has juggled a football across the longest distance, and has balanced a football on his head for the longest time. Can you guess how long he did them for?**

a) Ball-juggling distance:
   1) 2.1km   2) 5.3km   3) 10.4km   4) 21.2km
b) Head-balancing time:
   1) 1h 1m   2) 8h 42m   3) 24h   4) 73h 2m

10. **Why was the 2005 Sunday League match between Peterborough North End and Royal Mail AYL abandoned after one hour?**

a) Two giraffes that had escaped from a nearby zoo ran onto the pitch.
b) A bolt of lightning killed the referee.
c) The referee lost his temper and sent himself off.
d) The police showed up and arrested all Royal Mail AYL team on suspicion of stealing a mail van.

11. **How long did it take football fan Ed Wood to watch a league match at all 93 league stadiums in England and Wales in 2016 and 2017, which was the fastest time it's ever been done. (That's 20 Premier League clubs, 24 clubs each in the Championship, League 1 and League 2, and Berwick Rangers, which is in England but plays in the Scottish league system.)**

a) 93 days
b) 145 days
c) 189 days
d) 299 days

12. **Why did Ronnie Brunswijk, the 60-year-old vice president of Suriname, a country in South America, make the headlines in 2021 during a match between Inter Moengotapoe, from Suriname, and Olimpia, from Honduras?**

a) He sacked the coach during half-time, delivered the team-talk and spent the second half barking orders to the players from the side of the pitch.

b) He ordered the police to arrest the referee for awarding Olimpia a penalty he didn't agree with.

c) He played as centre-forward for an hour, making him the oldest person ever to play in an international club competition.

d) He made himself the referee, and gave five controversial penalties to Inter Moengotapoe.

13. **Both times that France won the World Cup, in 1998 and 2018, the team was known for a curious pre-match ritual. In 1998, captain Laurent Blanc kissed the bald head of keeper Fabien Barthez before every match. What did the squad do before each match in 2018?**

a) Touched Kylian Mbappé's nose

b) Stroked Adil Rami's moustache and beard

c) Tickled Paul Pogba's chin

d) Flicked Antoine Griezmann's ears

14. **What strange item did Argentinian fan Gabriel Aranda bring with him to join in the celebrations when his team, Racing Club, won the league title in 2019?**

   a) A pig tattooed in the team colours
   b) The skull of his dead grandfather, who was a huge Racing fan
   c) The ashes of his dog, Racey, who always wagged her tail whenever Racing played on TV
   d) A real-size replica of the trophy made entirely from his fingernails

15. **Who was Paul the Octopus?**

   a) A Manchester United goalkeeper famous for his amazing reach
   b) The charismatic founder of Barcelona who had amassed his fortune in the fishing industry
   c) A real octopus who correctly predicted the outcomes of all Germany's games in the 2010 World Cup
   d) The Italian coach who invented the 1-8-1 tactical formation

GERMANY RESULTS
2010 WORLD CUP
WIN   AUSTRALIA
LOSE   SERBIA
WIN   GHANA
WIN   ENGLAND
WIN   ARGENTINA
WI   SPAIN
         URUGUAY

16. **Argentinian goalkeepers often shout "*Kiricocho!*" just as a penalty is being taken at them, in the belief that it will bring them good luck. *Kiricocho* is ...**

   a) ... a phrase that means "pants on fire!"
   b) ... a mystical Patagonian falcon and the national bird of Argentina.
   c) ... the nickname of a fan who obsessively followed Buenos Aires club Estudiantes in the 1970s.
   d) ... the name of Argentina's goalkeeper in the 1986 World Cup who famously saved a penalty in the World Cup final.

17. **What did German coach Felix Magath tell his Fulham captain to put on his injured thigh to make it better (he was sacked by Fulham shortly afterwards)?**

   a) Dog wee
   b) Curdled cheese soaked in alcohol
   c) Leeches
   d) Black Forest gateau

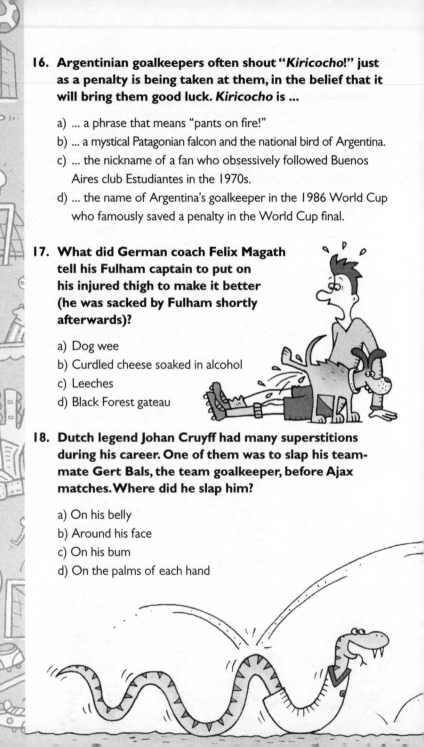

18. **Dutch legend Johan Cruyff had many superstitions during his career. One of them was to slap his team-mate Gert Bals, the team goalkeeper, before Ajax matches. Where did he slap him?**

   a) On his belly
   b) Around his face
   c) On his bum
   d) On the palms of each hand

19. You should never throw an object onto the p[itch]
fans around the world have not always taken h[eed of]
that advice. Which of the following items have be[en]
thrown onto the pitch during matches?

    a) Car door
    b) Cricket bat
    c) Wheelbarrow
    d) Live snake
    e) Pig's head
    f) Cabbage
    g) Tricycle
    h) Microwave
    i) Tennis balls

20. In 2019, a Premier League match between Everton
and Wolves was temporarily halted when what animal
invaded the pitch?

    a) Squirrel
    b) Cat
    c) Ferret
    d) Snake

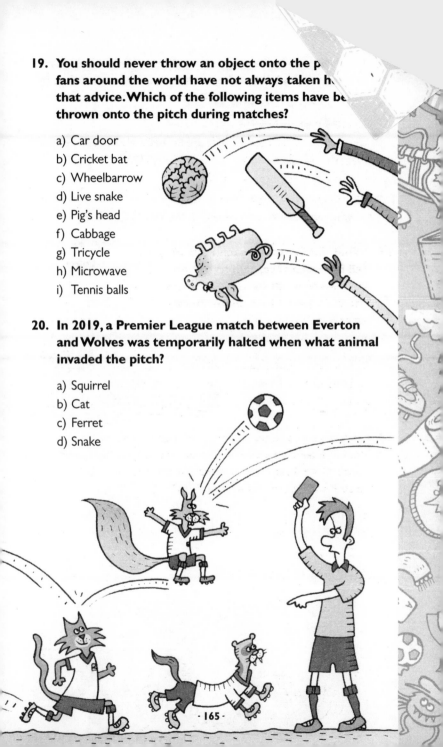

- 166 -

QUIZ ANSWERS

GLOBAL GAME

1. 1) Argentina, 2) Bolivia,
   3) Trinidad and Tobago
   4) Mexico, 5) Germany,
   6) Hungary, 7) Algeria,
   8) Egypt, 9) Oman,
   10) Ghana, 11) Liberia
   12), Laos 13) England
2. d
3. a
4. a, d, e
5. c
6. d
7. a
8. a) 9, b) 8, c) 7, d) 5, e) 1
   f) 10, g) 6, h) 4, i) 2, j) 3
9. c
10. d, a, d
11. a, b, d, f, g
12. d
13. a) 6, b) 5 c) 4, d) 3, e) 2, f) 1
14. a, c, b and d, c, b
15. b
16. a) 6, b) 5, c) 1, d) 2, e) 3, f) 4
17. b, e, d, a, f, c, g
18. b
19. b
20. d

GUTSY GOALIES AND DOGGED DEFENDERS

1. e, b, f, a, c, d
2. c
3. a) 6, b) 8, c) 9, d) 7,
   e) 10, f) 1, g) 4, h) 2,
   i) 3, j) 5
4. c
5. c
6. d
7. b
8. b
9. d, b, c, a
10. a
11. a
12. d
13. c
14. b
15. d
16. b
17. a
18. a
19. c
20. b

WHAT'S IN A NAME?

1. a) 9, b) 13, c) 2, d) 12, e) 4, f) 6, g) 1, h) 11, i) 7, j) 10, k) 3, l) 8, m) 5
2. b
3. a) 7, b) 1, c) 3, d)9, e) 2, f) 8, g) 10, h) 5, i) 4, j) 6
4. a
5. a) 8, b) 9, c) 1, d) 6, e) 4, f) 3, g) 7, h) 10, i) 5, j) 2
6. d
7. d
8. a) 2, b) 1, c) 4, d) 3, e) 9, f) 7, g) 6, h)10, i) 5, j) 8
9. c
10. c
11. b
12. d
13. a
14. a
15. c
16. a) 1, b) 5, c) 4, d) 2 e) 3
17. a
18. a
19. c
20. a) 4, b) 3, c) 2, d) 1

BALLS AND BOWLS

1. c
2. d
3. b
4. c, d, e, g, i
5. a
6. d
7. c
8. d
9. a
10. c
11. d
12. a) 6, b) 5, c) 7 d) 9, e) 3, f) 10, g) 4, h) 2, i) 1, j) 8
13. c
14. a) 3, b) 1, c) 2, d) 4
15. b
16. a
17. a
18. c
19. c
20. c

- 169 -

MARVELLOUS MIDFIELDERS AND STAR STRIKERS

1. a) 3, b) 8, c) 5, d) 9, e) 1, f) 2, g) 6, h) 4, i) 7
2. c
3. a) 10, b) 6, c) 8, d) 4, e) 7
4. c
5. c
6. d
7. a
8. d
9. a, d, f, j, m
10. d
11. b
12. b
13. d
14. d
15. a, d, f, g, i
16. c
17. a
18. a, d
19. c
20. d

TROPHIES AND TOURNAMENTS

1. a) Premier League, b) World Cup, c) Champions League, d) Women's Champions League, e) FA Cup
2. c
3. d
4. c
5. a
6. a) 10, b) 4, c) 8 d) 7, e) 6, f) 9, g) 3, h) 11, i) 2, j) 5, k) 1
7. c
8. b
9. c
10. d
11. b
12. b
13. c
14. c
15. b
16. b
17. d
18. b
19. a
20. a

SUPER STATS

1. d
2. a
3. a) 59, b) 25, c) 27
4. b
5. c
6. a
7. c
8. b
9. a) 54, b) 46, c) 55, d) 35, e)11, f) 10
10. a) 5, b) 4.5, c) 13, d) 3.5, e) 0.5, f) 4.5
11. b
12. d
13. a
14. c, a, d
15. d
16. c
17. a
18. b
19. c
20. a) 46%, b) 26%, c) 28%

CLEVER COACHES

1. a) 4, b) 7, c) 8, d) 6, e) 2, f) 3, g) 5, h) 1
2. d
3. c
4. d
5. c
6. b
7. d
8. e, b, d, a, c
9. c
10. d
11. b, d
12. d
13. a
14. b
15. b
16. b
17. c
18. d
19. d
20. a

CLUB CULTURE

1. a) 4, b) 2, c) 9, d) 5, e) 6, f) 10, g) 1, h) 7, i) 8, j) 3
2. English first division: a, c, e
   Scottish first division: b, c, e
3. c
4. a) 2 (Corsica), 7,
   b) 3 (Majorca), 9
   c) 4 (Madeira), 8,
   d) 5, 10 (Sicily),
   e) 1 (Zealand and Amager), 6
5. a
6. d
7. c
8. a
9. b
10. b
11. a) 1, b) 4, c) 2, d) 3, e) 5
12. a
13. c
14. c
15. a) 6, b) 4, c) 7, d) 5, e) 2, f) 1, g) 3
16. c
17. b
18. d
19. c
20. a

MOMENTOUS MATCHES

1. a) 6, b) 4, c) 3, d) 5, e) 2, f) 1
2. c
3. b
4. d
5. d
6. b
7. a) 5, b) 7, c) 6, d) 4, e) 3, f) 2, g) 1, h) 8
8. d
9. a
10. a
11. b
12. c
13. c
14. c
15. b
16. d
17. a
18. d
19. a
20. a) 2, b) 5, c) 3, d) 1, e) 4

RULES AND REFEREES

1. c
2. b
3. Goal: a, c, f, g
   No goal: b, d, e
4. b
5. a) 1, b) 5, c) 2, d) 3, e) 4
6. a
7. b
8. b
9. c
10. a
11. a
12. b
13. d
14. b
15. b
16. c
17. Direct: a, c, d
    Indirect: b, e, f
18. b
19. b
20. Real: b, d, f
    Fake: a, c, e

FABULOUS FASHION

1. a) 1, b) 4, c) 5, d) 3, e) 2
2. Foden: b
   Rapinoe: a
3. d
4. d
5. d
6. c
7. d
8. a) 8, b) 9, c) 4, d) 5, e) 3,
   f) 6, g) 10, h) 1, i) 2, j) 7
9. Lion: b, f, g, h, i, n, o, q, s, t
   Eagle: a, c, d, e, j, k, l, m, p, r, u
10. Real: a, c, d, g
    Fake: b, e, f, h
11. a) 5, b) 4, c) 3, d) 2, e) 1
12. a, c, e
13. d
14. b
15. c
16. d
17. a
18. c
19. a) 3, b) 4, c) 1, d) 2
20. a

LOVELY LINGO

1. b
2. a
3. d
4. c
5. a) 3, b) 2, c) 4, d) 1
6. Real: a, d, e, f
   Fake: b, c, g
7. c
8. d
9. a
10. d
11. a) 5, b) 4, c) 7, d) 2, e) 1,
    f) 6, g) 3
12. a) 3, b) 4, c) 2, d) 1
13. a
14. True: a, c, d, e
    Fake: b, f, g
15. a) 4, b) 3, c) 2, d) 1
16. a
17. b
18. a) 5, b) 1, c) 4, d) 3, e) 2
19. b
20. a) altitude b) petrified,
    c) stature, d) unanimous

KICKS AND TRICKS

1. d
2. d
3. a
4. a) 3, b) 4, c) 1, d) 2, e) 5
5. b
6. d
7. b
8. c
9. b
10. d
11. c
12. a
13. d
14. b, c, a
15. c
16. c
17. b, d
18. d
19. a
20. b

WACKY WORLD

1. d
2. d
3. c
4. b
5. a
6. c
7. a
8. d
9. a) 4, b) 2
10. c
11. c
12. c
13. b
14. b
15. c
16. c
17. b
18. a
19. a, c, e, f, i
20. b

The hidden word spells out:
THE GREATEST EVER

ACKNOWLEDGEMENTS

Time for one last question: who is the best illustrator in the history of football quiz books? It's Spike Gerrell! Thank you Spike for once again proving to be king of the cartoon. Big thanks to the team at Walker Books, especially Charlie Wilson, Daisy Jellicoe, Denise Johnstone-Burt, Louise Jackson, Laurelie Bazin, Maryam Rimi and Rebecca Oram.

We are grateful to our agents at Jankow & Nesbit and David Luxton Associates.

Finally, Ben would like to thank Clemmy and Bibi for test-driving some of these questions and Annie for her support and inspiration. Alex would like to thank Nat, Zak and Barnaby.

ABOUT YOUR COACHES

Alex Bellos writes for the *Guardian* and is the author of several bestselling popular science books.

Ben Lyttleton is an author, broadcaster and consultant to professional football clubs.

Spike Gerrell draws cartoons for magazines and books.

MORE FROM FOOTBALL SCHOOL